ALONG THE WATER'S EDGE

ALONG THE WATER'S EDGE

*Stories That Challenge
and How To Tell Them*

by Daniel Juniper

with a preface by
Morton T. Kelsey

PAULIST PRESS   *New York/Ramsey*

Cover art and interior illustrations by Gabriel Uhlein

Copyright © 1982 by   3-86
The Missionary Society of St. Paul
the Apostle in the State of New York

Library of Congress
Catalog Card Number: 81-84348

ISBN: 0-8091-2395-9

Published by Paulist Press
545 Island Road, Ramsey, N.J. 07446

Printed and bound in the
United States of America

CONTENTS

FOREWORD   *ix*

INTRODUCTION   *1*

STORIES FOR MINISTRY
   ONCE UPON A PUDDLE   *9*
   WALKING WITH THE LORD   *15*
   FOR THE LOVE OF A STREETSWEEPER   *20*
   A GLIMPSE INTO THE STABLE   *26*
   THE VERY LAST DAY   *30*
   THE PARABLE OF THE LIGHTHOUSE   *34*
   MARY AS JEWISH MOTHER   *39*
   A FATHER'S LOVE   *42*
   THE HAPPY MAN'S SHIRT   *47*
   LORD, WHEN DID WE SEE YOU?   *51*
   BARNABY THE JUGGLER   *55*
STORIES THAT BRING ALIVE THE SCRIPTURES
  MIDRASH
   ANANIAS THE SHOEMAKER   *63*
   THE PRODIGAL FATHER   *68*
   UNLESS A SEED DIE   *71*
   THE WEDDING STORY   *75*
  THE PARABLES
   THE GOOD SAMARITAN   *79*

v

THE RICH MAN AND LAZARUS   81
CHILDREN
A LITTLE BOY'S PENTECOST   85
ADVENTURES WITH JESUS   90
THE INNKEEPER OF BETHLEHEM   93
TELLING OUR FIRST STORY
APPENDIX
  I. STORIES FOR USE WITH THE SYNOPTIC
     GOSPELS   106
 II. STORIES FOR USE WITH THE SUNDAY
     LECTIONARY   110
III. RENEWAL PROGRAMS   114

Gratefully dedicated to all who shared the joy of the Mount experience, especially that first retreat team who, weekend after weekend, sat through the endless retelling of these stories: Christian, Juanita, Connie, Carol, Guy, and Sam.

"A number of theologians recently have become interested in the importance of stories. They sense that all our logical, scientific, and theological discourse is secondary. I share this belief. I have long thought that theology is to religious narrative as literary criticism is to literature—commentary upon a more basic form of expression."

> —Thomas Driver
> Professor of Theology
> and Culture
> Union Theological Seminary
> New York City

"What I wish y' could tell me, bein' an eddicated man an' all that, is why wit' all this eddication business about, they're very few good tradesmen an' story people left in the country, like?"

> —Mickey Ward
> tinker and storyteller
> Sligo, Ireland

Foreword

Storytelling springs out of the depth of the human soul. Before human beings knew how to communicate in abstractions and logic they were telling stories to one another. They communicated a great deal through stories. Through images and tales, they told of things which really mattered, of angels and demons, of gods, of creation, of destiny and life after the grave. They also passed on their folk wisdom through fascinating fairytales. Folktales conveyed psychological understanding.

Springing from a deep level of the soul, stories also touch that level and have an impact upon it. I remember very clearly the Seneca Indian legends my mother told me as a child. She had been touched by them and had recorded them with the help of my grandfather's interpreter. These stories gave me a feeling of brotherhood and understanding of Indians which I have never lost. My childhood friends would sit entranced by these stories.

I have discovered that people remember the anecdotes I tell far more than the five points that I have made or my careful arguments. They tell me that some story in a sermon or a lecture has really moved them, sometimes even changed their lives.

So often we forget how wise Jesus was. Not only was he the Son of God, he was the wisest of human beings. He knew the human heart and mind better than any person ever has. He was a superb psychologist and an expert in communication. And usually Jesus conveyed his message in parables, in stories. He used the most universal symbols, the very images which still occur in dreams. This is one reason why his message is always fresh and alive, never stale or outdated or dull.

But the Creator God is the greatest storyteller of all. He made the world in all its concreteness. He picked the Hebrew people and told the story of his love in the account of his dealings with them. When human beings still did not understand, he entered the story himself as a baby in a manger. He lived his story to a self-giving death on a cross and in resurrection. He wrote his story into the fabric of history in order to make it clear.

It is natural to tell stories, but modern Christians have undervalued storytelling and so have forgotten this native human art. In his excellent guide to storytelling, Daniel Juniper calls attention to what we are missing. He sent me this manuscript at the suggestion of a mutual friend. I was delighted with the material and the way it was presented. I suggested he send it to my editor at Paulist Press. Those at the Press agreed that here was a message which many people were looking for.

In the pages which follow Daniel Juniper provides a practical and useful guide to the use of stories in helping people understand the good news of the Christian Church. He gives clear, simple and excellent suggestions on how to get started in this neglected art. He offers us a group of stimulating stories to help us as we begin. These stories also open our eyes to the value of such tales. He points the way to finding other stories or creating them ourselves.

This book breathes a fresh, new spirit which can help many in the Church to reap the fields which are ripe for the harvest.

Morton Kelsey
Gualala, Cal.
Lent 1981

INTRODUCTION

The stories in this book have touched many lives.

Over ten years they have proven themselves in every conceivable situation—liturgies, retreats, classrooms, counseling sessions, and even family kitchens. These stories work. They draw people from behind their walls and challenge them to deepen their lives in the Lord.

Yet this book is more than just a storybook, for within its pages we can also learn *how* to storytell. But before I explain the unique simple approach of this book, let me tell you how I got started in this wonderful madness.

Ten years ago, I told my first story. And I can assure you that I was anything but prepared. My good friend Christian stood up in front of thirty people, announcing:

"I have a special surprise—Daniel is going to tell us a story!"

"*Me?* Tell a story? Where did you get that crazy idea?"

The eyes of the crowd flowed toward Christian, who quietly chuckled, "Now, Daniel, we only want a little story. You did a fine job when we walked alone in the woods. Tell that one about Brother Juniper when he gave away half of the church to the poor widow."

I ran my fingers through my hair in irritation. How could I tell a story in front of so many people? I'd never storytold in

1

all my life, except in passing. I'd just mangle it and make a fool out of myself.

"Now look, Christian, I'm not a storyteller."

But the others begin to side against me:

"Oh, come on, Daniel!"

"Don't be a stick in the mud!"

"You don't have to be perfect!"

After some more haggling, I finally gave up. At this point, you're probably expecting me to say that everything went wonderfully. Right? Wrong. When I first stood up, I felt as though I was pulling a long heavy freight train with a hundred boxcars. Each word jerked and creaked as I struggled to gain momentum. I stumbled over sentences. I even got the climax mixed up and had to repeat it twice.

When it was all over, I sat down in a back corner of the room, depressed. Now, when I'm enjoying my self-pity, I don't like to be disturbed. I like to savor it. So I was especially startled to hear a voice call out of the crowd:

"Hey, Daniel, tell us another story!"

The chorus grew.

"Yes, give us another!"

"Please—just one more!"

Good heavens, were these people masochists? What was happening? Amazed, I looked up to find a quiet expectant fire burning in their faces. Somehow, they had not noticed my many mistakes; indeed, they only wanted another story. At that moment, I began to suspect that the need for storytelling flows more deeply in the human heart than I had ever dreamed.

And so, ten years ago, while telling that first ragged story of Brother Juniper, faltering, groping, discovering, I seemed to row ashore onto a new and exotic land. In reality, I had discovered the oldest and surest way of communicating religious truth. I wound up much like the mixed-up English explorer of whom G. K. Chesterton speaks. Miscalculating his course, the

2

poor sailor discovered England under the illusion that it was a new island in the South Seas:

There will probably be a general impression that the man, who landed (armed to the teeth and talking by signs) to plant the British flag on that barbaric temple which turned out to be the Pavillon at Brighton, felt rather like a fool. I am not here concerned to deny that he looked a fool. But if you imagine that he felt a fool, or at any rate that the sense of folly was his sole or his dominant emotion, then you have not studied with sufficient delicacy the rich romantic nature of the hero of this tale. His mistake was really a most enviable mistake; and he knew it, if he was the man I take him for. What could be more delightful than to have all the fun of discovering South Africa without the disgusting necessity of landing there? What could be more glorious than to brace one's self up to discover New South Wales and then realise, with a gush of happy tears, that it was really old South Wales?

So it goes with storytelling. Though an adventure that thrills the twentieth-century American, it still proves more of a home-coming than a discovery. We forget the obvious. Long before the written word, storytelling was warming the fireside of the human heart. Certainly, our first attempts are a bit ragged around the edges, but I find that good storytelling flows out of human beings quite naturally—once they are given good stories to tell. That's the catch. Many storytelling books spend a hundred pages on technique and then throw a few story-examples into an appendix. This always seemed backward to me. The stories themselves come first. It's good stories that are hard to come by, not advice on storytelling. And it's knowing good stories that makes a person *want* to become a storyteller. Stories themselves can be the best teachers.

As you hold this book in your hand, you may mumble, "Make up your mind, Daniel! Is this book a collection of good stories for ministry, or a 'how-to-storytell' book?" I have to smile and answer, "Both, really." In the table of contents, our eyes fall on a section entitled "Telling Our First Story." Here we have a step-by-step explanation of how to prepare for storytelling. With it, the busy Christian can learn essentials in a short time. But notice that my section on how to tell stories lies at the back of the book, and is concise. Why? I find that lengthy discussions of technique—especially at the outset—can imperil the spontaneity from which storytelling flows.

Good storytelling stems from two simple things. First, we love a story. And then, we love someone else enough to share that story, in our own personal way. Technique is secondary.

In this book, the *stories are written to be told.* That may sound simple enough, but the written story and the oral story are two very different creatures. It proves difficult to translate a flowing oral experience onto a printed page. It is doubly difficult to write these stories so that the reader can easily translate them *back* into that original oral experience.

The following stories have a simple and direct style with a minimum of description. Transition passages, necessary in the ordinary written story, have not been added—these merely clutter the oral story, where a simple pause from the storyteller can do the job. And the incredible warmth of the human voice, face, and body add so much color to the oral story that it becomes a sore temptation to try to capture this magic on the printed page with excess verbiage. But for the sake of their telling, we need to keep these stories simple. As we read this book, we need to imagine them as being storytold, and *listen to them with our ears.*

Since dialogue is so important, it has been set apart from surrounding descriptions. The stories themselves are divided into units, helping the storyteller to easily grasp the main outline of the story. And, occasionally, type is set into verse to let us hear the rhythm of the spoken words. As an additional help to our imaginations, a few stories have an introductory paragraph that sets a scene where the story might be told. The appendix suggests many more practical settings for these stories' use.

And so, we stand holding this book in our hands. The decision we face is a simple one. Do we want to row ashore onto that forgotten land of storytelling or not? It is an exciting place to explore, though our first discovery might prove more surprising than we had ever dreamed. In our adventure, we just might stumble upon the footprints of a Galilean carpenter along the sandy shore. They say he loved to tell stories as he walked along the water's edge.

Welcome home.

Acknowledgements

As with any storyteller, my stories are a mixture of those that I have created myself, those adapted from friends, and those gathered from traditional sources.

"Unless a Seed Die" was adapted from a homily given by Father Donald Halpin, O.F.M.

"Mary as Jewish Mother" was adapted from a real-life anecdote first told to me by a friend.

"Walking with the Lord" was adapted from a meditation used by Father David Rosage of Spokane, Washington.

"Lord, When Did We See You?" is an adaptation of a homily given by an unknown Franciscan who shared his experience with Dorothy Day, co-founder of the Catholic Worker Movement. (All attempts to track down his identity have failed.)

"The Parable of the Lighthouse" is an adaptation of a short parable by Theodore O. Wedel in the October 1953 issue of *The Ecumenical Review.*

"A Glimpse into the Stable" is an adaptation from a real-life story found in Timothy O'Neill's *The Individuated Hobbit*, published by Houghton Mifflin Company. "On the Very Last Day," "The Happy Man's Shirt," and "Barnaby the Juggler" originate in traditional sources.

"The Prodigal Father" is based on a story in the appendix of Morton Kelsey's *The Other Side of Silence* (Paulist Press, 1976)

The excerpt in the introduction concerning the mixed-up English explorer is found in G.K. Chesterton's *Orthodoxy*, published by The Bodley Head, Ltd.

The epigrams at the beginning of the book come from *Patterns of Grace* by Thomas Driver, published by Harper and Row, Inc., and from *Our Like Will Not Be There Again* by Laurence Millman, published by permission of Little, Brown, and Company.

Special thanks go to my good friend, Bonnie Traughber, who patiently transcribed many of these stories from tape.

STORIES FOR MINISTRY

"On another occasion Jesus began to teach by the lake. The crowd that gathered around him was so large that he got into a boat and sat in it out on the lake, while all the people were at the shore along the water's edge. He taught them many things in parables. . . ."

Mark 4:1

ONCE UPON A PUDDLE

> "Then Jesus looked at him with love and told him, 'There is only one thing more you must do. Go and sell what you have and give it to the poor; you will then have riches in heaven. After that, come and follow me.' "
>
> Mark 10:21

It is Ash Wednesday, and as the minister steps from behind his large wooden pulpit, the congregation expects another typical Lenten sermon, exhorting them to turn back to God. Instead, he walks quietly to the altar steps. The gentleness of his first spoken sentence sharply contrasts with the explosiveness of the next three exclamations:

This is a story about some fishes who lived in a very small puddle of water.

"Give me that waterbug!"
"No, I saw him first!"
"Get your fins off my supper! He's mine, I tell you!"

And so, every day, the little fishes would fight. In such cramped quarters, there isn't much else to do—except swim

9

in circles and hunt for waterbugs. Their stagnant puddle was cradled between the roots of an ancient oak, just beside a swiftly-flowing river. Life never seemed to change for the puddle-fishes.

But one morning, as they swam in circles and hunted for waterbugs, there was a sudden noise:

SPLASH!

"Watch yourself!"

"Stand clear!"

An amazing, brightly colored fish had jumped into the riverside puddle! This large fish had blue and red and golden scales. And—what was *most* unusual for this particular puddle of water—he was smiling.

At first, the frightened puddle-fishes huddled together against the puddle's far edge. Finally, one of them asked:

"Where do you come from?"

The Sparkling Fish smiled brightly:

"I come from the sea!"

"The sea? What is the sea?"

The Sparkling Fish shook his head in surprise:

"No one has ever told you about the sea? Why, the sea . . . the sea is what fish are made for!" He rubbed a golden fin against his nose, puzzled:

"How can I explain the sea to you? Well . . . it isn't like this little puddle; it's endless! A fish needn't swim in circles all day, for he can dance with the tides. Life isn't lived in the shade—the sun arches over the waves in silver and crimson! And there are many splendid sea-creatures, such as can hardly be imagined.

"It's endless! And sparkling clear. The sea is what fish are made for!"

A waterbug skirted the surface overhead, but no one moved. Then a pale gray puddle-fish spoke up:

"How do we get to the sea?"

The Sparkling Fish pointed toward the large black root that lay close to the river's edge:

"It's a simple matter. You jump from this little puddle into that river and trust that the current will take you to the sea."

Astonishment clouded the puddle-water. At long last, a brave little fish swam forward with a hard experienced look in his eye. He was a Realist Fish.

The Realist Fish looked down at the muddy puddle-bottom and frowned:

"It's pleasant to talk about this 'sea-business' but—if you ask me—we have to face reality. And what is reality? Obviously, swimming in circles and hunting for waterbugs."

A look of distaste mingled with pity crossed his face:

"It's all pie-in-the-sea nonsense. Of course, I sympathize . . . you undoubtedly dreamed this up because of some trauma you suffered as a little guppie. But life is hard. It takes a real Fish to face facts.

The Sparkling Fish smiled:

"But you don't understand. I've *been* there. I've seen the sea. It's far more wonderful. . . ." Yet, before he could finish speaking, the Realist Fish swam away.

Next, there neared a fish with a nervous twitch in his tail. He was a Scared Fish. He began to stutter:

"If . . . I understand y-y-you, we're supposed to j-j-jump into that river over there?"

"Yes. For a fish who wants to go to the sea, the way lies through the river." The Sparkling Fish swam closer. (It is difficult to understand someone when he stutters underwater.)

The Scared Fish's voice jumped to a screech:

"B-B-But . . . have you looked at *that river over there?* I'm just a small fish! That river is deep and strong and wide! Why, a small fish would be swept away by the current! If I

11

jumped out of this puddle, I wouldn't have any control. NO! I just can't. . . ."

The Sparkling Fish whispered:

"Just trust me. Trust that the river will take you someplace good. . . ." But before he could finish, the Scared Fish hurried away.

Finally, there swam out a figure who seemed very solemn and learned. (He had been in this particular school of fish longer than anyone else.) He was a Theologian Fish.

Calmly, he swam to the middle of the puddle and adjusted his spectacles. Setting down a small shellfish podium, the Theologian Fish pulled out a sheaf of notes from his vest pocket. Then he smiled at the puddle-fishes:

"My brothers and sisters, our distinguished visitor has expressed many views which certainly merit consideration."

Then he bowed respectfully to the Sparkling Fish:

"However, my colorful friend, we must also concede that those fishes who so gracefully inhabit this humble puddle have expressed many views which merit consideration. By all means, let us be *reasonable*."

He glanced down at his notes, and then his smile brightened:

"We can work this out. Why not form a discussion group? We could meet every Tuesday at seven o'clock, and I'm certain that some of the puddle-fish would be happy to bring coffee and donuts. . . ."

The eyes of the Sparkling Fish were sad:

"No, this will never do. Talking is important, but in the end—it is a simple matter. You jump. You jump out of this puddle and trust that the river will take you to the sea."

From somewhere above the muddied waters, a sparrow was singing. The light in the Sparkling Fish's eyes shone with a bright urgency:

"Besides, don't you know? Summer is coming!"

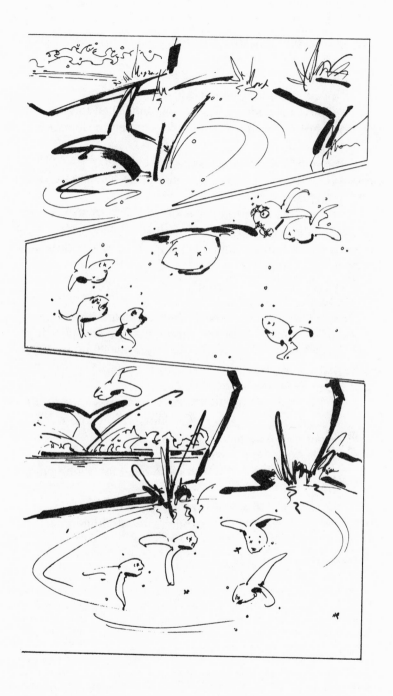

The puddle-fishes murmured:

"Summer is coming?"

"What difference does that make?"

The Sparkling Fish pointed toward the sun:

"Summer is coming. The spring rains filled this little puddle to overflowing. But this puddle is going to dry up someday. No puddle lasts forever."

The puddle-fishes were stunned, but then the Realist Fish swam out. There was a dark contempt on his face as he spat out his words:

"That's just like you religious people. When you don't honestly convince people of what you believe, you try to scare them. You're just one of those end-of-the-puddle fanatics!"

He swam away in disgust.

But then all the colors of the Sparkling Fish—blue, red, and gold—brightened into a warm glow. He whispered:

"It is a simple matter. You jump from this little puddle, and trust that the river will take you to the sea. Who will come and follow me?"

At first no one moved, but then a few puddle-fishes swam to his side. Together they jumped into the river, and the current swept them away.

The remaining puddle-fish were quiet for a long time.
Then once again
they began to swim in circles
and hunt for waterbugs.

WALKING WITH THE LORD

> "Come to me, all you who are weary and burdened, and I will give you rest."
>
> Matthew 11:28

It is the first evening of a weekend workshop on Christian prayer, and the retreat master looks out at twenty-five eager faces. Many are typically American faces: tense, serious, ready to work hard at making a significant breakthrough in their prayer life. Some chew nervously at the ends of their pencils, waiting to take notes.

The retreat master gives a relaxed smile and then begins his story:

One bright autumn morning, I was sitting at my breakfast table, thinking:

"I've certainly had a lot of problems lately. Troubles at work, troubles at home. . . . I really ought to take time to pray about them."

But then, all of a sudden, I sensed that someone had

walked into the room behind me. I turned around and gasped:

"Lord Jesus! What are You doing here?"

The Lord Himself was standing in my doorway! I rubbed my eyes—was it really He? Yes, everything checked out . . . from the tip of the white seamless robe to the faint glimmering halo around His head. I stammered:

"That is . . . errrr . . . it's not that You *shouldn't* be here. I'm just not used to You dropping by in such a visible form."

This unexpected visit had unsettled me, and I vaguely wondered if I had done anything wrong. He smiled and the light in His eyes grew brighter:

"Would you like to go for a walk?"

"Uhmm . . . why . . . sure!"

And so, we walked down the little country road that leads past my home. Slowly, the truth began to dawn upon me and I murmured to myself:

"What an incredible opportunity! He has all the answers to all my problems—my relationships at work . . . my worries about the future . . . my family problems. All I need is to ask."

We walked quietly for several minutes, and then I turned to Him:

"Excuse me, Lord, but I need some advice on this very difficult problem . . ."

But before I could finish, He had raised His fingers to His lips:

"*Shhhh*. . . . Do you hear it?"

At first, I didn't hear a thing. But then came the faint tumbling of a nearby brook, crisp and light beneath the autumn colors. The Lord sighed:

"Isn't that beautiful?"

"Ah . . . yes . . . I suppose so . . ."

I was thoroughly distracted. (He had interrupted my train of thought.) I waited a few minutes to show due respect, and then—just as we walked past a rolling meadow—I blurted out:

"Lord, I've been worried about my prayer life. Things have been awfully dry. Now, according to the books that I've read—"

He put His arm around my shoulder:

"*Hush* . . . do you hear it?"

Children were running through the meadow grass. Once again, He smiled:

"Isn't it wonderful?"

"Uhmm . . . yes . . . now that You mention it."

Then I added irritably:

"You know I love children."

We walked on. A horrible thought loomed in my mind—what if I lost this opportunity? Here were all the answers to all my problems, right at my elbow! He even knew the deepest mysteries of the universe—love . . . death . . . the Armageddon! As a last resort, I thought I'd talk to Him about religion. After all, that *is* His line of work:

"Lord, I was wondering what You think of the conflict in modern biblical scholarship between . . ."

Again, the friendly arm came around my shoulder and I gritted my teeth. The Lord stopped and silently picked up a roadside pebble. He grinned:

"I'll bet you can't hit the top of that telephone pole."

I was bewildered. Why, of all things! And from the Lord! (This was not what I had expected from the Second Person of the Holy Trinity—if you were God, wouldn't *you* be a bit more serious about it?) He casually tossed His pebble toward the pole:

It arched silently through the air.

Hmmmm.

He missed!

My depression was deepening, but still I stopped to pick up a pebble. What else could I do? Half-heartedly, I tossed it

17

in the general direction of the telephone pole:

It arched silently through the air.

Hmmmm.

I hit it!

The Lord proudly looked at me and chuckled:

"Hey, you're *good*."

As we strolled on, the knots in my stomach grew tighter. Whenever I wanted to talk about anything of any importance, there would always be an interruption. Some faded blue chicory would be brushed by the wind, or a butterfly would light on a moss-covered fencepost.

Note: At this point, the storyteller shifts to present tense, to intensify the immediacy of the story's last line, which is delivered looking directly into the eyes of the listeners.

At last, our walk is finished. I am so upset that I can think of nothing to say. Beneath His long black beard, the Lord has a playful smile, and as He turns to leave, the light in His eyes grows brighter.

He walks to the door, and then stops to glance at me over His shoulder:

"Stop trying so hard."

For the love of a
Streetsweeper

Once upon a time, there lived a poor streetsweeper named Sam.

He lived in a time of splendor and chivalry, when shining knights battled dragons beneath a golden sun. Unfortunately, Sam only knew such splendor from afar. Each morning he would awaken in his shack and look into the cracked mirror that hung on his wall:

"Lord, the day you made me—you certainly made a mistake."

The townsfolk agreed. His face appeared a haphazard arrangement of floppy ears, a long crooked nose, and sad brown eyes. By itself this was bad enough, but whenever Sam opened his mouth, his words would become tangled beyond

20

repair. The lonely streetsweeper lay awake on summer nights, watching the stars through a hole in his tin roof. He sighed:

"If only I were someone else. Perhaps a merry troubador who sings in the marketplace, or even a page for a great knight. If only I were anyone . . . anyone but Sam . . ."

Hot July days would be the hardest because the dust raised by his broom would stick to his skin, while bored children ran behind him in the streets:

"He's scared of his own shadow!"

"If I looked like him, I'd be scared too!"

Sam bowed his head and kept sweeping.

One day, just as the sun dropped below the castle walls, the little streetsweeper was cleaning a particularly dirty alley. He was grumbling:

"Why can't folks put the lids on their garbage cans . . . Oh!"

Someone had suddenly tapped Sam on the shoulder. The startled streetsweeper turned around and saw the son of the castle's lord standing at the entrance to the alley! The Prince asked:

"Who are you?"

Sam took a step backward and bowed.

"W-w-why, I'm Sam, the village streetsweeper."

The Prince looked at the battered garbage cans. Then he looked at Sam.

"These old alleys must get lonely sometimes."

"Y-y-yes, sire."

Then the Prince began to smile:

"Sam, there's something about you that I like. How would you like to be my friend?"

Sam dropped his broom and stuttered:

"W-w-what did you say?"

The Prince's smile grew:

"I like you, Sam."

And so, the strange friendship began. Sam was not the

only one bewildered—the entire city was in confusion. Ladies in the castle courtyard whispered:

"Why would the Crown Prince want a friendship with such an ugly nobody?"

But still the friendship grew. The pair took walks along the castle moat and rode together in the woods. They hunted mushrooms in the spring and blackberries in the fall. And then, slowly, the streetsweeper began to change.

At long last, he grew happy to be Sam.

One bright day, the Prince said:

"Sam, I have good news. I'm going to be married in the spring, and I want you to come as a guest of honor."

Sam floated on a cloud, as though he were a young knight who had just slain his first dragon. He had never been invited anywhere, much less to the wedding of a prince. But then Sam looked down at his clothes and the happy cloud turned dark:

"What can I wear? A torn tunic and a ragged pair of overalls? . . . I'll have to get a second job and earn the money for a wedding suit."

And so Sam got himself a town-crier route. He tumbled out of bed before daybreak and walked the streets:

"Hear ye! Hear ye! Hear all about it! Sir Lancelot rescues damsel in distress . . ."

And so, many weary months later, Sam brought home a beautiful new wedding outfit. He carefully tried it on. It had a white shirt and white coat and white pants and white shoes and a white tie, not to mention a pair of white suspenders with imitation diamonds which spelled: "S-A-M."

The happy streetsweeper had never seen himself look so distinguished.

The winter months dragged by, but at last the wedding day came. Sam pulled out his rusty washtub and scrubbed himself clean. Then he put on his white shirt and white coat and white pants and white shoes and white tie, not to mention his white suspenders with imitation diamonds that spelled: "S-A-M."

He breathed a sigh of satisfaction:

"I had better be going. After all, I *am* a guest of honor."

But when Sam opened his door, he got an ugly surprise. Black clouds were tumbling across the sky. He moaned:

"How will I *ever* get to the wedding without the storm ruining my beautiful white wedding suit?"

Sam had no choice. He huddled beneath an old ragged umbrella and stepped out into the rain. Somehow—without a spot of mud splashed on his white wedding suit—the street-sweeper ran all the way to the great castle.

And then, a great awe settled over him.

In the dark night, the castle was radiant with life. Through its jeweled windows, Sam could see chandeliers blazing with crystal. The wedding guests danced across glittering floors dressed in gold and silver and satins. It took Sam's breath away and he felt afraid:

"Does a streetsweeper belong at such a feast? I don't even know how to dance . . ."

But then he shook himself:

"Still, my friend the Prince *did* invite me."

Sam crouched beneath his torn umbrella and stepped toward the castle drawbridge. But suddenly his foot slipped:

"Arrrrrrrgggghhhhhhhhh!"

SPLAT.

Sam had fallen—head-first—into a gigantic mud-puddle. He staggered to his feet and looked at himself. (Oh, misery!) Now Sam had a brown shirt and brown coat and brown pants and brown shoes and a brown tie with a brown pair of suspenders. His imitation diamonds spelled absolutely nothing at all. He tried to cheer himself up:

"Well, at least they still match."

But this only made him feel worse. The splattered street-

sweeper had worn his best, and now his best was dripping with mud. He turned to go, but the memory of his friend's invitation rose to his mind:

"Sam, I have good news. I'm going to be married in the spring, and I want you to come as a guest of honor."

His foot hesitated.

Will Sam go into the wedding feast?

Would you go into that great castle, dripping with mud?

A GLIMPSE INTO THE STABLE

"For God so loved the world that he gave his one and only Son, that whoever believes in him should not perish but have eternal life."

John 3:16

Paul stared at the fireplace but he could feel his wife's rising anger. She called through the kitchen doorway:

"Why can't you go with us to Christmas services?"

He sank into his leather armchair and sighed:

"Gail, I don't want to argue about it. You know that I believe in God. But as for God ever becoming Man—that's something which I just can't understand. It just doesn't make sense to me."

Nothing more was said. She dressed their little boy and then drove away from the farmhouse, the car headlights outlining birches against the winter sky. Heavy snow lay on the ground. Even for Vermont, it was a bitterly cold night.

Paul threw some pine into the fireplace and became lost in his thoughts:

"Christians claim that God has become Man. Yet, why

would the infinite God of the universe do such a thing? Even if it were possible, it doesn't make sense . . ."

Note: At this point the storyteller can smoothly shift to present tense, heightening the sense of immediacy, drawing the listeners more fully into the story.

But suddenly, there is a sickening thump on the window-pane. Paul gives a startled glance out into the night:
"What's going on out there?"
A flock of birds has gathered, drawn by the warm light of the house. As they flutter on the deep snow, their wings begin to freeze. Paul opens his front door—the little birds are so miserable that he *has* to do something. But he shakes his head:
"They'd never come into the house . . . they'd be too frightened."

Though the wind is empty of starlight, Paul can still see the shadow of the old vacant stable-house that lays across the farmyard. Lantern in hand, he walks across the snow and swings open its door:
"It's not much. But at least you can get out of the wind."
He circles from behind and shoos the birds toward the stable-house. But they scatter across the barnyard, a confusion of fluttering shadows. Paul mutters irritably:
"Come . . . I'm not trying to hurt you. Can't you understand?"
He opens wide the doors of the stable-house, hanging the yellow lantern-light in an empty stall. Again Paul waves the birds toward the stable and again they scatter across the snow.

Paul stands helpless in the cold:
"They'll freeze to death. If only they knew that I'm trying

to save them. They would understand me, if only I could become one of them . . .''

He looks at the frightened dying birds and then glances upward. A gulf in the clouds has unveiled a single white star just above the lantern-light of the stable.

Silently, Paul understands.

Then he bows in the snow
   before starlight
         before stable-light
         and before the God who has become Man.

THE VERY LAST DAY

> "Therefore keep watch, for you
> do not know the day or the hour."
> Matthew 25:13

The teacher walks into the classroom and welcomes the fifteen adults who sit in a circle of folding chairs. It is the first weeknight session of a program entitled "A Deeper Understanding of How Christians Live."

A few of the men sit dejectedly beside their wives, their downcast eyes plainly saying: "I wouldn't be here if she hadn't dragged me. . . ." The teacher breaks the ice with introductions and, as the mood relaxes, gently begins:

There once lived a man in ancient Spain whose days were every bit as busy as yours. One day his shop was overflowing with customers, when a good friend dropped by:

"I have good news, Felicio!"

The merchant dropped a heavy roll of satin from his shoulder:

"It had better be important, friend. The store is mobbed, and I hardly have time to chat."

His friend winked an eye:

"It *is* important. You once told me that you have a burning question within your heart, one which you have shared with no one."

"That is true. There is no one to answer it with wisdom."

"Well, I have heard news of a great saint who lives along the southern coasts. Now you have someone to ask the question."

The merchant stared out the shop door—the moment had finally come. He gently pushed the astonished customers out the door, saying:

"Please . . . an emergency has arisen . . . come again some other day . . . I'll have to close the shop now . . ."

And so, the eager man set out with a rugged pilgrim's staff. Throughout the long barefoot journey, through fields and mountains, the question burned more deeply into his heart. At last he found himself beside the saint's seaside hut. When the door swung open, a small elderly man stood smiling:

"Good morning! Come in and have some tea. . . ."

But the pilgrim answered:

"I have one question to ask of you, and I'll not budge until it's answered."

The saint leaned against the doorpost and waited.

"If you had one day to live—just one day—how would you spend that day?"

The old man stroked his long white beard:

"Well, first I might say my morning prayer . . . Afterward, I might fix a little tea and go out to weed my garden . . . Of course, I might go down the road to visit my neighbor Juan, since his arthritis really bothers him this time of year . . ."

The old man paused to watch some gulls dive into the nearby waves.

". . . Then I might have a bite of lunch . . . or perhaps I'd take a nap . . ."

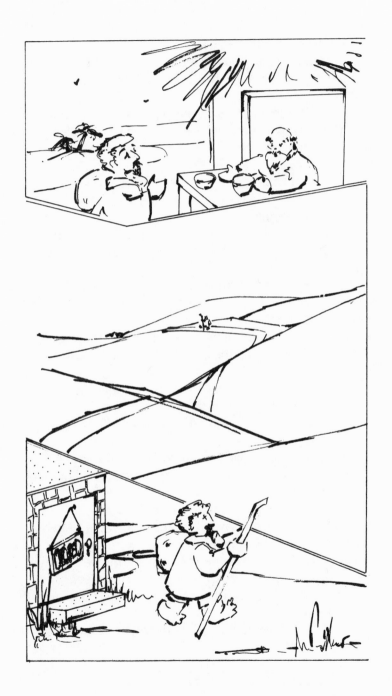

The pilgrim stopped his words:
"Wait! That's the way you live every day."

There was silence as another gull plunged into the water. The old man smiled:
"Of course. Why would I live my last day any different-ly?"

THE PARABLE OF THE LIGHTHOUSE

> "You are the salt of the
> earth. . . . You are the light of the
> world. . . . Let your light shine before
> men that they may see your good
> deeds, and praise your Father in heaven."
>
> Matthew 5:13-14

The two men stood on the high cliffs.

"What do you think, John?"

The other man listened to the night and answered:

"With the wind pounding the waves against those rocks, it's hard to tell. But I'm afraid we have another one."

The first man shook his head:

"Aye, and it's the third shipwreck this month. I'd best tell the crew."

He ran down the beach to a small lighthouse and pounded on the door:

"Time to be moving! There's a wreck up near the north cliffs. We heard the cries in the wind."

The life-saving crew tumbled out of the lighthouse, their sea-worn faces pale in the lantern-light. They plunged their little boats into the waves with amazing skill.

Such tragedies often struck that lonely coastline. A sudden shift in the winds, a thick fog rolling across the water, a treacherous turn in the tides—and an unlucky ship would slam into the sharp reefs, its hull slashed by the rocks.

The cry would go out:

"Abandon ship!"

But no sooner had these words left the captain's lips, than the lantern of a life-saving boat would appear in the darkness, leading the wrecked seamen to safety.

The little lighthouse soon grew famous. Each day, it seemed, there came a new knock on the door:

"I've come to help!"

"You saved my son's life. Please take this small sum, a sign of my gratitude."

"I want to be part of your crew!"

The ramshackle buildings were repaired. Large boats were built and crew members traveled to schools for professional training. Then one day, the entire crew sat in a circle on the sandy beach and held a meeting. A young man stood up and said:

"What are we waiting for? Everyone knows that this old lighthouse isn't meeting our needs! We need bigger and better facilities!"

Everyone shook his head in agreement. Soon the old structure had been torn down and a sparkling new lighthouse rose above the beach. And, as their fame grew even wider, a luxurious wing was added onto the new white tower.

In it, the newly-formed Lighthouse Society could celebrate its social functions.

The years fled by. Then one rainy night the Society was holding its annual formal dinner. The guests were dining by candlelight and dancing to a string quartet when suddenly:

"Look, a red flare over the sea!"

The cruel rocks had trapped another victim. As the dinner continued, the rescue crew fought the storm in desperate relays. This shipwreck proved the most horrible of all. There had been an explosion aboard ship, mangling many of the survivors. They flooded the lighthouse, filling the ballroom with confusion and overturning tables. The dinner guests were stunned.

Many of those shipwrecked were naked and hysterical. Worst of all, some even had black or yellow skin.

The lighthouse's governing committee met in emergency session. The annual dinner—vital to their fund-raising efforts—had been ruined. There was ugly murmuring:

"Something must be done."

And so separate buildings were constructed for shipwreck victims, in order that the new lighthouse would not be soiled nor the social functions of the Society be disrupted. But soon other problems arose, and at last the chairman of the lighthouse called a general meeting:

"Times have changed. This lighthouse has grown and taken over many new and important functions. The old work of life-saving is now a hindrance to our tasks."

An angry debate followed and a minority protested:

"But we are a rescue station!"

"If we stop saving lives, we have lost our reason for existence!"

Yet they were shouted down. When the ballot was taken, the lighthouse had discontinued its life-saving operations.

An angry minority left in protest and moved to a rocky reef down the coast. In the midst of great hardship, they built a new lighthouse. Over the years, the fame of this new little lighthouse spread, until one day there arrived a delegation of benefactors:

"Such a courageous crew deserves more than a dilapidated lighthouse. We have raised funds for an entirely new building. . . ."

A modern lighthouse soon arose into the air, and professional crews began to battle the tides. Then, with the passing of time, life-saving operations became less and less frequent.

Again members divided into bitter factions. Angry argument flared into the open, and a few left to build a third lighthouse. So it was with a fourth lighthouse, and a fifth, and a sixth . . .

Until today, there are many expensive and exclusive lighthouses along that stormy coast.

Many are the ships that wreck upon its cruel rocks,
and many are the lives
that are lost.

Mary as Jewish Mother

> "I reared children and brought them up, but they have rebelled against me. The ox knows his master, the donkey his owner's stable, but Israel does not know. . . ."
>
> Isaiah 1:1-3

The old priest sat uncomfortably in his chair. The retreat master asked him:

"What has happened in your prayer time?"

The man cleared his throat:

"Well, not much, really. . . ." There was an embarrassed silence and the frustrated director thought to himself:

"The retreat is going nowhere. This fellow has drifted so far from God, nothing seems to work."

But then a memory rose in his mind, and he turned to the old man:

"Last evening you were telling me about those days when you first studied for the priesthood. When you felt distant from God, you would sit and talk with Mary, and she would show you how to come closer to the Lord . . ."

The old priest shook his head and interrupted:

"Yes . . . but that was years ago. One grows out of such things."

The retreat master smiled:

"Well, I want you to do a special meditation. Just imagine dropping by Mary's house for a cup of coffee, and let's see what happens . . ."

Several hours passed. The director was sitting in his office when suddenly the old man stood in the doorway. His face was alive with light. Obviously, there had been a breakthrough.

"What happened in your meditation?"

The white-haired priest smiled:

"I did exactly as you said: I imagined myself walking through the streets of Nazareth. Mary lived in a small clay house near the village well. I knocked on the little door and waited."

He chuckled to himself, and the retreat master leaned forward:

"Well—what happened?"

The light in the old man's eyes grew:

"It was like coming home to my own mother. I waited . . . and then footsteps came. When the door opened, Mary stood wiping her hands on her apron. She looked at me and said:

" 'And where the hell have you been?' "

A FATHER'S LOVE

> "How great is the love the Father has lavished upon us, that we should be called children of God! Yet, that is what we are."
>
> John 3:1

The week-long youth camp is drawing to a close. As the youth minister walks toward the podium, the teenagers gather on benches in the outdoor amphitheater. Tonight climaxes five days of busy activity. Now the young people will be invited to deepen their relationship with God.

Before beginning the evening's talk, the minister walks into the crowd of teenagers:

Every evening after supper, Carol would go to her room and turn on the radio. And it never failed: just as her favorite song came on the air, her father would appear in her doorway.

"Carol, have you done your chores yet?"

And she would cross her arms and say:

"Why do I have to do all these stupid chores? I'm not a child anymore—I'm sixteen years old!"

Carol had her father's gray eyes, but not a touch of his quiet temperament. When she had finished screaming, he would softly say to her:

"Get on with your chores."

There was dishwashing and cooking and sewing—but most of all Carol hated the yard work. She was expected to prune and water the rosebushes which her father had planted against the house.

Carol did her work, but only because it was her duty.

One morning in early March, she trudged through the snows of a nearby pine grove. Gathering firewood was the last thing Carol wanted to do. Yet here she was, tracking through the slush behind her father's muddy boots:

"What a way to spend a Saturday . . ."

Her father turned around and said:

"Stay here, Carol, while I go to the creek and look for windfalls."

He was gone a very long time. At first Carol kept her eyes downcast on the melting snow. But when she finally looked up, there was a surprise waiting—a large uprooted pine hung suspended over her head. Its wide arms had snagged long ago on the branches of a nearby hemlock, leaving it suspended above the forest floor. Carol eyed the tangle of branches. If she pulled the lowest limb, the entire tree might topple to the ground. She said to herself:

"That tree has a lot of good firewood."

Carol tugged for several minutes, and at last she heard a high-pitched creaking sound. The tree was ready to fall. She yanked with all her strength—but suddenly she hear a voice from behind:

"*Carol!*"

It was her father's voice. Her anger simmered:

"He probably wants me to carry something that *he* found. And just when I've almost got this tree down."

She ignored the call and pulled the tree all the harder. It gave a low groan, and in the branches overhead there was a sharp crack. Again the voice came—though this time much closer:

"*CAROL!*"

Suddenly she was thrown to the ground in a tangle of branches. There was a muffled thud. Through the twisted limbs, Carol could see her father's red jacket beneath the huge trunk.

An expert woodsman, he had seen how the tree would twist when it fell.

Her father had thrown her out of the way, but he wasn't able to get out of the way himself.

With each day that her father lay unconscious, the doctors had less and less to say. In the antiseptic hospital corridors, they whispered over their steel charts, and Carol lay awake each night, waiting for the return of her mother's car, ready for the certain news.

Then one spring morning her mother stood at the bedroom door. Without looking up, Carol knew what she was going to say. As her mother's footsteps quietly crossed the floor, Carol closed her eyes.

Her mother whispered:

"Carol . . . Daddy woke up."

She flung her arms around her mother:

"He *woke up!*"

Carol was a dancing blur of tears as she ran from the room. Her mother called:

"Where are you going?"

"To the hospital."

She ran downstairs and out onto the front porch. Then, just as her feet reached the sidewalk, Carol caught sight of something climbing against the red bricks of the house.

It was the first rose of spring, flowering on one of her father's rose bushes. Without losing any momentum, she spun

around and snatched the white blossom. Then she ran down the sidewalk to the hospital.

A half a mile later, Carol ran past an astonished receptionist:

"Young lady, it's not even visiting hours . . ."

But before she could finish, the teenager was gone. Carol ran up four flights and spilled the breakfast trays that an orderly was carrying down the stairwell:

"Hey, kid! Where do you think you're going!"

But before he could finish, she was gone.

Carol burst into her father's room, but abruptly stopped just past the doorway, as though she had unexpectedly come to the edge of a high cliff. She fumbled with the flower in her hands. Would he be angry? But when she looked up, his gray eyes were smiling at the rose.

Joy,
laughter,
tears.

Carol ran to her father's arms. Something deep inside had changed.

Now she would gladly prune her father's roses forever, if only to see him smile.

The happy man's shirt

"Blessed are you poor, for yours
is the kingdom of God."

Luke 6:20

Once upon a time there was a wise and gentle king. The entire realm prospered under his kindly hand, but one day sad news spread through the land:

"His Majesty is very ill, and no one knows if he will recover."

The court physicians hurried to the royal bedside, but none of them could work a cure. Wise men from the far corners of the realm passed through the castle gates, each with a special remedy. Yet the king only grew worse, and a dark gloom settled over the countryside.

But then one morning a strange old man wandered into the castle courtyard. His eyes were bright and his beard was long. There was a weathered mandolin flung over his back. When he saw the sadness on every face, he turned to a small page boy:

"Why are there no smiles in this land?"

The page whispered:

"Our king is very ill, and no cure can be found."

The old man stroked his white beard and laughed:

"Ah, but there *is* a remedy for the king. He only needs to wear the shirt of a happy man!"

These words reached the ears of the court ministers, and in desperation they sent out an urgent decree:

"It is hereby ordered by His Majesty's Royal Council that the shirt of a happy man be procured for the health of His Majesty the King."

So the search began.

Of course, messengers were first sent to the nobility, for who enjoyed more pleasures than the lords of the kingdom? But—lo and behold—the search failed.

Their wives constantly nagged them for more jewelry, and their children disobeyed their every word. Even when the nobles sent their sons to the finest schools for knighthood-in-shining-armor, the grade reports were appalling. And then, each lord spent sleepless nights worrying about his forests, his fields, and the spiraling demands of the serfs' union.

There was no time to be happy.

Next, the royal horsemen looked among the merchants. Certainly within the solid middle-class there lived a happy man, for they had neither too much nor too little. But—lo and behold—the search failed.

As the economy recessed into recession, the merchants depressed into depression. The price of porridge skyrocketed to five shillings. A bottle of mead hit an all-time high. And the price of fuel soared—one pound four shillings for a single bale of hay! Desperately, the merchants spent all their spare time trying to gain favor at court and thus win themselves a title.

Among the entire middle-class, there was not to be found a truly happy man.

At last the messengers came to their senses:

"Of course! The peasants! They live hearty lives that are

uncluttered with complications. There must be a happy man among them!"

But alas, this venture was also doomed. The peasants grumbled about high taxes as they organized bitter protest demonstrations against their landlords. When they brought home their wages, their wives complained that it was not enough—and when they went on strike for higher wages, their wives complained that they brought home nothing at all. Among all the peasants, there lived no truly happy man.

The dark gloom deepened across the face of the land.

The search had failed.

Then one morning, the crown prince went hunting in the royal forests. He and his companions had stopped their horses near a dense thicket when—from its far side—there came a strange voice. It was unlike any voice they had ever known, for it was truly happy:

"Ah, I've had a crust of bread, a slice of cheese, and a bite of fruit. I can't think of anything more that I could want. *I'm perfectly happy.*"

The crown prince tightened his fists on the reins of his horse. He turned to the other hunters and said hoarsely:

"*I want his shirt. Take it by force if you must, but I want that man's shirt!*"

The horsemen spurred their mounts around the thicket. They swept toward an old dilapidated hut, an odd collection of straw and mud and branches. The men leapt off their horses and kicked open the front door, splintering it into pieces.

A small ragged man sat smiling at them.

Lo and behold!

> The man was so happy
> > and so poor
> > that he didn't even have a shirt.

LORD, WHEN DID WE SEE YOU?

> "Lord, when did we see you hungry and feed you, or thirsty and give you something to drink? When did we see you a stranger and invite you in, or needing clothes and clothe you? When did we see you sick or in prison and go to visit you?"
>
> Matthew 25:37-39

She looked like anybody's grandmother.

Stephen had been seeing a friend on the psychiatric ward when an aide whispered:

"See that visitor who just walked in? That's Dorothy Day."

Stephen turned to find a small elderly woman standing at the next bed. Her hair was tied in a neat white bun and she wore a vintage-1940 flowered dress. He thought to himself:

"What's so remarkable about her? Is this the famous modern-day saint who works with the poor?"

She looked so ordinary. Still Stephen introduced himself and asked if he might accompany her on her rounds. Dorothy Day quietly took his arm, and they strolled from bed to bed, chatting with each patient. Out of the corner of his curious eye, Stephen watched quietly.

Suddenly there was a loud scream. In the doorway, three orderlies struggled with a new patient. The woman's hair was tangled and ugly red scratches scarred her face. As she raged, she spit on the three men.

Stephen instinctively moved his arm to guide Dorothy Day away—just as he would any woman his grandmother's age—but it felt as though he were pushing against a rock. Her eyes were fixed on the screaming woman. The attendants dragged her into a padded cell and slammed the door. Then they limped away to nurse their wounds.

The woman kept shrieking.

Dorothy Day walked to the nurses' station and said:

"I want to go in there."

The head nurse smiled to herself and never looked up from her chart. She smiled:

"Take it easy, ma'am. If you keep talking like that, we might ask you to stay here awhile . . ."

By chance, a doctor walked onto the ward. Dorothy Day turned to him and quietly said:

"I want to go in there."

At first he ignored her, but then the physician made his mistake—he looked into her eyes. Something in those eyes held him fast. After an awkward moment of silence, he shrugged his shoulders:

"Nurse, have her sign a statement releasing the hospital of any responsibility. If that's what she wants, then let her go in."

The woman was clawing the walls when the cell door swung open. Though a dark viciousness twisted her face, her eyes were strangely blank. She tensed to leap upon the elderly figure who stood in the doorway.

Dorothy Day quietly held out her hand.

The woman fell back confused, and Dorothy Day stepped into the center of the cell. Seconds dragged into minutes and the woman's screaming slowly subsided to a hoarse whimper. Huddled in the far corner of the little room, she watched the outstretched hand, waiting for it to draw back.

Dorothy Day quietly held out her hand.

A long time seemed to pass. Slowly . . . very slowly . . . the woman reached out and touched the waiting hand.

When they left the hospital, Dorothy Day searched Stephen's face:

"Did you see him?"

Stephen was confused:

"Did I see him? Whom do you mean?"

She smiled gently:

"Jesus . . . there was nobody else in that room."

Barnaby the Juggler

"As he looked on, Jesus saw the rich putting their gifts into the temple treasury. He also saw a poor widow put in two very small copper coins. 'I tell you the truth,' he said, 'this widow gave more than all the others.' "

Luke 21:1-3

Early in the morning, the poor juggler would walk into the marketplace with an armful of colored balls and pins. He would roll out a tattered carpet and announce with a dance:

"Ladies and gentlemen, my name is Barnaby. Today I will give you my best and juggle with all my heart. Will you allow me the pleasure?"

And—in a flash—the air came alive.

Balls and pins.

Spinning, soaring, swirling!

He bounced them on his nose and on his toes!

The crowds would cheer and throw pennies onto his ragged carpet. Then he would gather up his small wage and wander to the next town. It was a hard life. When the village lamps grew dark and Barnaby lay under some lonely hay-stack, an emptiness overwhelmed him:

"Surely there is more to life than wandering about the earth, juggling balls and pins . . ."

Then one fateful day, Barnaby caught sight of a barefoot man in a long coarse habit. Dropping his balls and pins, he asked:

"Sir, could I become a brother in your monastery?"

The monk's eyes grew skeptical:

"Perhaps . . . but what is behind you on the ground?"

Barnaby turned around and pretended surprise:

"Oh! These? Err . . . nothing important . . . only a few balls and pins."

The monk frowned:

"A juggler, eh? Well, my son, that must go. Such worldly amusements are not proper for a man of God."

Reluctantly, Barnaby gave up his juggling. As much as he loved to toss his balls and pins, the repentant juggler wanted to follow God even more.

After a long year of trial, Barnaby was accepted into the monastery. He worked hard, but since the little man knew no practical skills, he was given the lowest jobs in the community. He cleaned the kitchen and swept the church and trimmed the vines which choked the monastery walls.

As the years passed, Barnaby grew closer and closer to the Lord.

Then one snowy Advent, the abbot ordered each monk to prepare a special birthday gift for the infant Jesus. By the time Christmas Eve arrived, Barnaby felt miserable. What could he possibly give to the newborn Lord? At evening prayer, each brother laid his present before the life-sized manger scene. One monk set down a fine wood-carving. Another brother sang a beautiful melody from the choir loft. Still another, kneeling in the chapel sanctuary, laid a magnificent scroll before the straw of the stable.

But Barnaby had nothing to give . . .

Later that evening, when all the monastery was dark and quiet, there exploded a sudden pounding on the abbot's door:

"Quickly! Get up! Oh . . . it's terrible!"

The abbot stumbled out of bed:

"What is wrong?"

The shaken voice of the gatekeeper spoke from the shadows:

"Brother Barnaby has gone mad! Quickly! Come to the chapel!"

And pulling the abbot by his nightshirt, the gatekeeper ran through the dark halls. The chapel door had been locked from within, so they had to climb the steps of the choir loft. Below, the church floor was lit by a single white candle, and in its dim flicker stood Barnaby. He had rolled out a tattered carpet before the life-sized manger. The lonely little figure bowed:

"My good Lord . . . ladies and gentlemen of heaven . . . my name is Barnaby. Tonight I will give you my best, and juggle with all my heart. Will you allow me the pleasure?"

And then—in a flash—the air came alive.

Balls and pins!

Spinning, soaring, swirling!

He bounced them on his nose and on his toes!

The gatekeeper threw a leg over the railing of the loft and started to climb down:

"He's gone quite mad. We must stop this sacrilege!"

But then the two monks gasped.

A stunning white light flooded the chapel. Balls and pins crashed to the flagstones, and the startled juggler froze before

the altar. In the midst of the lifeless manger, something stirred in the straw.

A baby was smiling from His crib.

Then the vision faded and Barnaby stood beside the flickering candle. The abbot cleared his throat:

"Ahhmmmm . . . we seem to be intruding . . ."

They quietly walked out the door and left the happy juggler alone with his Lord.

STORIES THAT BRING ALIVE THE SCRIPTURES

MIDRASH
Stories That Grow from the Scriptures

From ancient times, Jews have used the word of God as their primary take-off point for storytelling. Considering the central place that the Scriptures have had in their life, this is hardly surprising. They simply took their biblical insights and wove them into the real fabric of life. Such stories formed an essential part of *midrash,* Jewish commentary on Scripture. Indeed, such storytelling was quite common among rabbis of Jesus' time. Perhaps the most famous example is the parable of the Good Samaritan; with it, Jesus is merely making a midrash on the familiar quote from Deuteronomy commanding us to love God and our neighbor.

Ironically, for all their supposed legalism, the ancient Jews still felt the freedom to handle Scripture with imagination. It's a shame we haven't done the same—apparently, it was one of Jesus' favorite ways of teaching.

Maybe we should take the hint.

ANANIAS THE SHOEMAKER

> "In Damascus, there was a dis-
> ciple named Ananias. The Lord called
> to him in a vision:
> " 'Ananias!'
> " 'Yes, Lord,' he answered."
>
> Acts 9:10

The small church overflows with people on the cool June morning. All eyes follow the new minister as he steps to the pulpit to preach his first sermon. He looks out over their faces—theirs is a small church in a small town with a small congregation. He begins his story quietly:

Along a cobble-stoned alley of ancient Damascus, there once lived a shoemaker named Ananias. Like others of his scattered nation, the little cobbler went to his synagogue each week to pray for the birth of the Messiah:

"How long, Adonoi? How long is a little while?"

But then one Shabbat evening, some Galileans arrived at the synagogue door. Though dusty and tired from their long desert journey, the newcomers lifted their hands high above their heads:

"Brothers! We bring glad news! God has raised Jesus of Nazareth from the dead, that we might return to God!"

There was an ugly silence. One of the scribes murmured:

"The chief priests of Jerusalem have sent word: 'Beware of rabble-rousers who claim that a poor crucified carpenter is the Messiah!'"

Then an old man stood up:

"You are a disgrace to the people of Israel!"

Ananias sat on his crowded workbench and watched the porters throw the men outside. A great sadness crept over the little shoemaker—when would the Messiah come? He slipped out the back door and found the Galileans lying in a nearby gutter, laughing. Ananias suggested timidly:

"If I were you, I might not be so happy to be tossed into a gutter."

One of the men wiped a gash on his forehead and smiled:

"Now that the Messiah has come, I wouldn't mind being tossed head-first into a manure pile."

There was something about these men that the poor shoemaker liked.

"Tell me more about this Messiah . . ."

And so, after he had listened, Ananias became one of the brotherhood.

What an exciting time to live—the news of the empty tomb still rang freshly in the ears of men and women! With each passing day, new miracles broke through:

"Did you hear? Joseph the weaver has believed in the Messiah, and his whole family has received the Holy Spirit!"

"Incredible news! The blind man who begs by the old stone well—he can see!"

Yet, miracles never visited Ananias. He stitched strips of leather on his workbench and mused:

"After all, I'm only a simple cobbler who can hardly read the alphabet. A shoemaker must be content to sew sandals for the glory of God . . ."

Ananias' times of prayer were also very ordinary. There were no startling revelations—only a quiet gentle Presence.

But then one noontime, just as he set down his awl, something very unusual happened. A whisper rose within his heart:

"Ananias!"

The startled shoemaker tripped over his workbench. Then he remained still on the clay floor and listened to the silence, but the only sound was the wild pounding of his heart. But just as its beat began to calm, the voice came again:

"Ananias!"

This time the little cobbler knew who had spoken. He glanced upward:

"Here I am, Lord."

The voice came with a deep quiet authority:

"Arise and go to Straight Street, and at the house of Judas ask for a man from Tarsus named Saul. He will be praying. In a vision he has seen a man named Ananias. You are to place your hands on him so that he may see again."

Ananias winced. Forgetting to whom he spoke, the poor cobbler scrambled to his feet:

"Lord! Many people have told me about this man, about all the terrible things he has done to your people in Jerusalem. And now he has come to Damascus to arrest anyone who even calls upon your name!"

There was a long silence. Ananias looked upward:

"Lord?"

Silence. The shoemaker awkwardly shuffled his feet and cleared his throat:

"Ahem . . . Lord?"

Ananias sighed and bowed his head. Then the voice spoke again:

"Go, because I have chosen him to be my servant, to carry my name to Gentiles and kings, and to the people of Israel. I myself will show him all that he must suffer for my sake."

Ananias stumbled down his dirty alleyway. As in a dream, he wandered toward the wealthiest quarter of Damas-

65

cus. Then the shoemaker knocked timidly on the door of Judas and waited until the huge gate opened a crack. A skeptical servant peered out.

Ananias pushed past him with a clumsy dive:

"Please, sir! I must see a man by the name of Saul!"

At first the servant was startled by the frantic little shoemaker, but he quickly recovered:

"See here! The servants' entrance is around the back . . . of all the nerve!"

He planted his palm squarely in Ananias' face and pushed the poor man out toward the street. The struggling cobbler screamed:

"No! I must splee a man by the nab of Salb . . . Pleeb, I musk splee . . ." (It is difficult to be articulate when someone has his hand in your face.)

Just as the servant slammed the door, Ananias swung his leg into its path. This actually worked in the shoemaker's favor, since the volume of his screams markedly increased. They echoed throughout the neighborhood:

"AHHHHHHHHGGRRRR! My leg!"

Then there came a deep troubled voice from the inner courtyard:

"Wait! I had a vision about that man!"

Ananias panicked and forgot everything:

"Oh, no! . . . He had a vision about me! Now I'm *really* in trouble . . ."

The angry servant grabbed the shoemaker's belt and jerked him back into the courtyard. There, under an aging olive tree, a sightless man lay on a mat. The shoemaker's fear quietly melted away:

"Saul, I have been sent by the Lord Jesus whom you met along the way. He sent me here that you might see again and be filled with the Holy Spirit."

Ananias reached out for the sightless eyes. For a quiet

moment, human history rested beneath the hands of a cobbler.

When it was finished, a man named Saul had become Paul.

Some time passed before Paul began his ministry, and many more years fled by before the world realized its tremendous impact. And so, the little shoemaker never knew what came of the day when he stretched out his hands beneath that aging olive tree.

At the very end of his life, Ananias lay on his death bed. He looked upward to the desert skies and whispered:

"I haven't done much, Lord. A few shoes sewn . . . a few sandals stitched . . . But what more could be expected of a poor cobbler?

But then, once again, that same voice rose quietly within his heart:

"Don't worry, Ananias, about how much you have done—or how little. You were there when I wanted you to be there.

> *And that,*
> *my little shoemaker of a saint,*
> *is all that really matters."*

THE PRODIGAL FATHER

"We love because he first loved us."
John 4:19

In a far land over the sea, there lived a father who deeply loved his son. But the young man grew proud and ungrateful. And so, breaking his father's heart, he demanded his inheritance and went off to a foreign city where he could pursue his own pleasure. There he spent every penny on drinking and prostitutes and gambling.

But one gray morning after a drunken brawl, the young man awoke on a hard stone floor. He whispered hoarsely:

"Where am I?"

The lad struggled to his feet, only to find himself in a small locked cell. As panic closed in, he shook the bars of his cell:

"For God's sake, where am I? Let me go!"

The jailer sauntered down the hall, disgust on his face.

"You're not going anywhere, you filth. You probably don't remember what happened last night. You killed someone in a brawl—a perfectly innocent man. But we have ways of dealing with scum like you. Don't worry, the judges won't keep you waiting. They'll set the date of the beheading—and soon."

The young man sat down on his dirty straw bed, head in hands. He stared at the empty walls and counted the days until the execution.

In the meanwhile, the boy's father climbed a high hilltop every evening. With every sunset, he hoped to catch a glimpse of his returning son, but months passed and still his boy never appeared. Finally, in desperation, the father set out in search for him.

When he at last came to the city of his son's downfall, the father sought his son from tavern to tavern, from brothel to brothel. A disgusting trail of evidence led straight to the prison where the young man lay trapped.

The day of the beheading was only a few mornings away.

In his sorrow, the old man was allowed to visit the prison cell, but the son refused to even look at his father. Instead he curled up in the corner and refused to say a single word. In guilt and shame, he pushed the father away. The old man whispered:

"You are still my son."

But the young man only put his hands over his ears.

The father went to the judges and pleaded:

"Please, is there anything that can be done?"

They only shook their heads.

"No, there were too many witnesses. Justice must be done. He must die."

Bent with grief, the old man turned to leave. But then one of the judges put his hand on the father's shoulder:

"There *is* only one slim possibility. We have an ancient law in this land that a condemned man may be freed and forgiven if someone else will offer his life in the place of that criminal. There is no other way. But who would offer his life for such a useless creature?"

The father bowed his head.

"He is still my son."

Thus, on the appointed day, the old man climbed the steps to the executioner's block. And no sooner had the ax fallen than the young man heard his prison cell swing open. Once again outside the city gates, his eyes blinking in bright sunlight, it broke in upon him, only too late, how deep was his father's love. Broken-hearted, he stumbled along the dusty road that led toward home.

On his journey, the son met a ragged beggar. In days past he would have avoided such a lowly stranger, but now his life had changed, for he knew himself to be the poorest of the poor. The lad shared his bread with the ragged man and together they journeyed along the road. Many times tears choked the young man, and the stranger would listen silently to his tale of failure and debauchery and sin.

At long last, their path led to the doorway of the father's house. The young man turned to say goodbye to his friend, but suddenly the beggar smiled and held out his arms. He gently spoke the lad's name.

The son let out a gasp of disbelief, for the stranger was revealed to him: his father, risen from the dead!

For in that faraway country which had claimed the father's life, an even older law had restored it. According to the deep magic from beyond the dawn of time, those who give their life, expecting nothing in return, cannot truly die. And so the father had risen from the dead.

Together, they embraced as father and son, rejoicing in their new life. Now they could begin to share their deepest love. A great shining feast was celebrated—a double feast, giving thanks for the son set free, and for the father risen from the dead.

Unless a seed die

> "I tell you the truth: unless a kernel of wheat falls to the ground and dies, it remains only a single seed. But if it dies, it produces many seeds."
>
> John 12:24

The following unfolds as a dramatic monologue with a small amount of simple pantomime.

The storyteller lifts one hand high over his head and closes his fist as though grabbing a tree limb. His knees briefly bob up and down, simulating the motion of the branch. The eyes of the storyteller-turned-seed come to rest on an imaginary branch:

"Good morning! It's good to see a bird again. What did you say?"

The seed listens for a moment.

71

"What am I? I'm a seed . . . just a little seed hanging around, holding onto this tree limb. And—I might add—I'm not about to let go, either."

He pauses again, as though interrupted.

"How old am I? Well, now that you mention it, I'm exactly one year old today . . . though please don't feel you have to get me a card. It was a fairly easy delivery—my flower just popped right out of the bud! What a beautiful spring that was! With sunny days and warm evenings . . ."

Again interrupted, the storyteller-seed glances up at the bird.

"What's that? . . . I don't look well? A bit withered? Hmmmm . . ."

His face shows wounded vanity, but this is quickly clouded by confusion.

"I must confess—lately I haven't been feeling very well. And my hand *is* getting awfully cramped holding onto this branch . . . My problems really began last September when a night wind rose out of the north. Brrrrrr. It sent shivers right up the back of my pod!

"When I woke the next morning, the leaves were tinged with orange and red and yellow. And then—oh, it was horrible! My brother and sister seeds began to lose their grip. One by one, they fell to their death . . ."

As his eyes follow an imaginary seed plummeting to the ground, the storyteller-turned-seed imitates the scream of the plunging seed:

"AHHH
HH
HH
H
E
E
E
E
E
E
E."

He shakes his head, as though waking from a nightmare.

"Dear God, it was horrible. But there was nothing I could do—I told them not to let go! What else could I do? . . . But at least that isn't going to happen to me. No! I'm never letting go!"

He clutches the branch with growing desperation as he listens to the bird.

"What did you say? . . . Oh, yes . . . yes . . . I've heard that nonsense before—a seed falls to the ground and is born into a new life. My dear sparrow, do you really believe that? After all, this *is* the twentieth century."

He again listens to the bird, and his turmoil increases.

"Yes . . . yes . . . I know that I'm withered, and I know that life isn't worth living this way. But what else can I do?"

His face registers horrified shock.

"*Let go?* Are you *crazy?* Have you looked at how far I would have to fall?"

The storyteller-seed glances downward and shudders, as if on the edge of a dizzying precipice. He shuts his eyes and shakes his head.

"It's easy for you to suggest. You can fly! But I'd be killed! No! I'm not letting go!"

As he clutches the limb, the seed listens with growing pain.

"Yes . . . I know I'm not happy this way . . . and yes . . . I really don't have anything to lose . . . yes . . . perhaps you're right . . . perhaps I should let go."

He begins to loosen his grip, but then sucks in his breath and clutches the limb all the more desperately.

"No! I can't do it!"

But after a few moments of silence, his fear passes to resignation.

"Yes, I know you're right. I've got to let go . . . life isn't worth living this way. Oh God, help me . . ."

The storyteller-seed lets go of the branch and slowly squats down. After a few moments of silence, he stands, gracefully lifting his open hands. He looks at his firmly-planted feet and upraised arms in quiet amazement.

"What has happened? I have roots . . . I can grow!"

THE WEDDING STORY

"Another one said, 'I have just gotten married, and for this reason I cannot come.' "

Luke 14:20

The young man and woman sit together at the meadow's edge. She asks:

"What is troubling you, my love?"

At first, the young man does not answer. But then she kisses him on the forehead and he sighs:

"Just . . . something a friend said the other day."

He lies down, his head in her lap, his dark eyes watching the sun slip below the nearby cypress. The young woman traces his black hair with her fingers:

"And what did your friend say?"

"Oh . . . he was only teasing. I really shouldn't let it bother me. I was working in the shop when he came in and said:

" 'Now you've gone and done it, old man! You're going to be a family man—with a wife and babies to look after! Things will have to change. It'll be time to get your head out of the clouds! Your high ideals will change . . .' "

The sun has set and the shade of the thin cypress is woven into the dusk. Again the young man sighs:

"Some things should never change."

She gives him an embrace:

"What things, darling?"

"Well . . . you know what the Scriptures say: " 'You shall love the Lord with all your mind, and your heart, and your neighbor as yourself.' It seems *that* shouldn't change."

She smiles:

"I don't intend to change it."

The young man laughs:

"Well, now I know why you want to marry me—the fellow everyone calls a crazy idealist . . . But, my love, what about our children? If we love God with all our hearts, life won't always be safe . . . We'll have to take risks . . ."

As night shadows crouch beneath the trees and wait for the day to gather its last light, her eyes grow sad:

"For a woman to risk her child—it's unthinkable. And yet, I know one thing: unless we love God with all our hearts, we'll be hurting our children far worse than the world could ever hurt them."

The night shadows have crept out into the meadow. The two are quiet in each other's arms, and then he kisses her:

"Now, my love . . . just what are you thinking about?"

She smiles:

"Oh . . . I was just wondering . . . wondering what things God might have in store for our life, Joseph . . ."

"Who knows . . . who knows, Mary? But there is a very ancient saying:

'To those who truly love
God comes in a special way.' "

STORIES THAT BRING ALIVE THE SCRIPTURES

THE PARABLES
Confronting Them in Our Daily Lives

I once heard a scholar remark, "We can have an incredible technical mastery of the Bible, but in itself that means little. Ultimately, one thing really counts—do we let the Scriptures confront our daily lives?"

Especially with the parables of Jesus, that question hits home. Seldom do we allow them to challenge our lives with their blunt uncomfortable truths. Of course, we *talk* a great deal about them. And we *theologize* about them. But we seldom *tell* them.

The following stories translate the parables of Jesus for the modern world. Their technique itself is nothing new. Clarence Jordan pioneered it many years ago with his *Cotton Patch Gospels.* But his technique for paraphrasing Scripture has been little used, perhaps because it has been little understood.

The following parables are *not* an attempt to say: "This is the way it is, folks. This is Absolute Truth." Rather, they should be seen as experiments. No modern adaptation of Jesus' parables could be a perfectly tailored fit—but then, that would be impossible.

In one regard, however, the following parables perfectly reflect the original intention of Jesus. At the very least, he wanted us to ask hard questions about the basic assumptions of our lives.

THE GOOD SAMARITAN

> "I tell you the truth, the tax col-
> lectors and prostitutes are entering the
> kingdom of God ahead of you. . . ."
>
> Matthew 21:31

*The teacher looks out over the crowded cafeteria tables:
the faces are sprinkled with a healthy cross-section of the
parish. For once, she thinks to herself, the Lenten program
has been well-publicized in the bulletin.*

*"Tonight, as part of our preparation for Easter, we are
going to try an experiment. I am going to tell a story, and
I'm certain that you'll recognize the Gospel parable from
which it comes. Now, as I tell it, I don't want you to merely
accept my version as Gospel truth. But I want you to ask:
How closely does this story come—or how closely doesn't it
come—to what Jesus originally intended?"*

*She steps toward their tables, takes a deep breath, and
says a silent prayer. (Something on the order of: "Lord,
please don't let them throw their ashtrays at me. . . ."*

Then she begins.

Late one night, a certain man was driving home from a
Billy Graham crusade. As his car passed through the inner

79

city, its engine suddenly sputtered and died. There lay nothing for many dark blocks but crumbling boarded-up storefronts.

"What a terrible place to have car trouble . . ."

The streets were completely deserted. The man began to search for a pay phone, and his steps hurried whenever he passed a darkened alleyway.

Suddenly he felt a sharp pain in the back of his shoulders. As his legs crumbled underneath him, rough cruel hands dragged the man into the black alley. There was the muffled thud of a steel pipe, and through the spinning numbness he dimly felt someone reach into his pocket.

Then quick footsteps faded down the alleyway.

Now by chance there was a Catholic priest driving down that street after celebrating Mass downtown with the archbishop. When his headlights caught the figure of a man crawling toward the gutter, he mumbled to himself:

"It's likely a trap—those muggers often lie down in the street so that someone will stop . . ."

And he sped on.

Next there came a Protestant minister returning from a week-long revival. When he caught sight of the man crumpled in the gutter, he murmured:

"That's what comes of these people and their alcohol. It's disgusting. If only they would straighten up their lives . . ."

He also drove on.

Finally a certain homosexual was driving down that lonely street. When he saw the man lying unconscious on the curb, he was filled with heartfelt compassion. He pulled his car alongside and tore up his shirt for a bandage. Then he lifted the man into his back seat and sped through the darkened streets to a hospital.

There he signed papers accepting financial responsibility for the man's treatment, should he prove without insurance.

Then the homosexual went on his way.

THE RICH MAN AND LAZARUS

> "Woe to you who are rich, for you have received your comfort. And woe to you who are well-fed, for you will go hungry."
>
> Luke 6:24–25

There once was a middle-class American who lived in a suburban home with a two-car garage. And barely three hours away by airplane, there lived a poor man named Enrico.

Though Enrico worked very hard for a banana plantation, he could never make enough to feed his family. He would gladly have eaten from the garbage cans of the American, but whenever there came a collection for the missions, the American would only throw in twenty dollars, saying:

"That's really pretty generous. After all, money is tight. I can hardly afford to make the payments on my new car."

Years passed and finally Enrico died of malnutrition. He walked through death's door and found himself in Light, rejoicing with Abraham and the angels. The American died from a heart attack one day and was buried. He found himself in a cold empty darkness, utterly separated from God.

81

When he looked up, the American saw Abraham with Enrico at his side. He cried out:

"Father Abraham! Have pity on me and send Enrico here to give me just a little spark of warmth in my cold darkness. I can't stand this awful loneliness!"

But Abraham answered him:

"Remember, my child, that in your lifetime you lived in the wealthiest country in the world, while Enrico starved in poverty. But now he is enjoying himself here, while you are in pain. But besides, there is a deep abyss which separates us, so that no one can get across."

And so the American said:

"Well, then, I beg you, Father Abraham, send Enrico to my old suburbs, where my family and friends live now. Let him warn them so that they won't come to this place of pain and loneliness."

But Abraham only said:

"Those in your suburbs have Moses and the prophets. They even have Jesus. Let them listen to what these say."

"That's not enough, Father Abraham. But if someone were to rise from death and go to them, then they would turn from their selfishness."

"No, my child. Someone has already risen from the dead, and they did not listen to Him. It would do no good to send another."

Stories That Bring
Alive the Scriptures

CHILDREN
The Scriptures Brought Alive for Their World

Within the last fifty years, the Church has largely viewed storytelling as a kindergarten activity. Christians have forgotten the powerful impact that storytelling can have upon those of us with a few gray hairs. Hopefully, this book has helped to correct that misconception.

Still, it would be a mistake to ride the pendulum to the opposite extreme and entirely neglect the little ones. The psalmist boldly proclaimed: "Behold, children are a gift of God. . . ." That proves especially true with storytelling. As beginners, we can find no more enthusiastic audience for our craft. And with their blunt honesty, children will tell us exactly what works and what doesn't work. Children can prove an invaluable part of any storyteller's education. Next to stories themselves, they can be our best teachers.

Here follow a few examples of how the Scriptures can be brought alive for the world of the child. These stories are meant to spark the beginning storyteller's imagination. The possibilities for such techniques are as vast as the Scriptures themselves.

A LITTLE BOY'S PENTECOST

"In the last days, God says, I will pour out my Spirit on all people. Your sons and daughters will prophesy, your young men will see visions, your old men will dream dreams."

Acts 2:17

Once upon a time, there lived a shepherd boy named Ben.

He wandered with his family in a desert of red sand, helping his father watch their sheep. Often Ben would guard the flock at night, and that can get lonely—especially if there's no one to talk with except your pet goat. Still, Ben always tried to start a conversation with Zelpha each night:

"Well, how are you tonight, Zelpha?"

"Baaaaaaa," the black and white goat would answer.

"Err, has anything interesting happened lately?"

"Baaaaaaaa," she'd answer, twitching her tail.

"Don't you ever have anything to say except 'baaaaa'?"

"Baaaaaaaaa."

Life can get lonely, especially when you have to talk to someone who never has much to say.

Sometimes Ben would look up at the desert stars. The

sky looked so big and so full of bright constellations that the boy shepherd would feel very small—and very unimportant. Then he would try to imagine how much bigger God must be than the stars—and Ben would feel even smaller. At times like that he cheered himself by playing a tune on his shepherd's pipe . . .

One cold morning Ben knelt next to the fire and warmed his hands. He wanted to go back to bed, the way some of us feel on a gray Monday morning just before the school bus comes, as we stare into our bowl of cereal. He felt just like a soggy cornflake.

But suddenly his father walked into their tent:

"I have good news, Ben! We're going to Jerusalem for the great feast of Pentecost!"

Ben jumped up and down for joy. Jerusalem! Oh boy, Jerusalem! He had heard all about it. A giant city surrounded by big stone walls! Bright colorful caravans! Princes! And even the holy temple of God!

For the impatient little shepherd boy, the days seemed to drag on forever. But finally it came time to leave. The family packed up their tent and put it on camels, much in the way we pack up our station wagon to go camping. Then they rode several days across the sandy desert until (at last!) they saw the gates of Jerusalem.

Jerusalem! It was everything that Ben had imagined, and even more, with the big stone walls, the colorful crowds of merchants, the bright market places and, towering above everything else, the holy temple of God!

The family pulled up their camels in front of Uncle Mortechai and Aunt Bertharim's home and after about ten minutes Ben thought he would go crazy. No playing was allowed inside the house. (Something might get broken.) And no playing was allowed outside the house. (Uncle Mortechai didn't like noise.) They sat in the living room for about a hundred hours and listened to Aunt Bertharim complain about the price of garlic. Nobody wanted to sightsee. What a bore!

But the day before Pentecost, their cousin Simon burst into the house. They hadn't seen him for years, and now, for some reason, he called himself Peter. He brought along a bunch of his friends and announced that he had become a follower of some rabbi from Nazareth. The whole thing didn't make much sense to Ben. This rabbi—Jesus by name—had been a very good man. Yet the police arrested him and put him on trial. Then they executed him for treason. But even that wasn't the hardest thing to understand. Peter claimed that Jesus had risen from the grave and had promised to send them his Holy Spirit!

The grownups talked far into the evening and soon Ben fell asleep in his father's lap.

Early the next morning, cousin Peter woke everyone up:

"Happy Pentecost, everyone! The time has come for the Lord to send his Holy Spirit, just as He promised! Let's go upstairs and wait for His gift!"

Everyone crowded up the stairs. Ben was the very last, but just as he had climbed halfway up, his older cousin Jonathan turned around:

"And where do you think you're going, half-pint? You can't come up here—you're just a kid. Go on, now! Why don't you go outside and play in the street?"

Ben's face turned bright red. He clenched his fists and stomped down the stairs, kicking the living room wall with all his might.

"Just a kid! That dumb cousin Jonathan! He thinks he's such hot stuff!"

But then Ben noticed something: everything was very quiet upstairs. The little shepherd boy looked at the empty stairs and giggled:

"I know what I'll do! I'll just sneak up there—they'll never notice!"

He climbed the stairs carefully (oh so carefully!). He mustn't make a sound or—

CREEEEEAK!

87

Ben winced. Rats, the stairs were made of old creaky wood!

On his tiptoes, he again crept up each stair, one by—

CREEEEEEEEAK!

Ben closed his eyes and sucked in his breath. No one stirred in the room upstairs. With a few more steps, he found himself standing in front of the upstairs door. He slowly turned the doorknob and the door began to move. Easy does it—

CRRREEEEEEAK.

Ben bit his lip: the door had rusty hinges! He slowly opened it a little more and now he could see the grownups through the crack in the doorway. They all sat around a large wooden table, quietly praying with their eyes closed. Their hands were open in their laps. All at once, Ben realized that if he was going to do something, he had better do it quickly. And so—as fast as he could—he snuck across the room and dove under the table!

Thump-a-thump-a-thump-a-thump: his heart was racing a mile a minute! The little shepherd found himself next to Aunt Bertharim's feet, and suddenly two thoughts flashed through his head:

"I made it! Boy, I really made it!"

But as he looked at Aunt Bertharim's feet, another thought came to his mind:

"Ooooh, no—if they catch me now, I'm in trouble. Big trouble!"

That was the last thing Ben remembered thinking before the tornado hit the house.

Suddenly a mighty wind swept through the room and almost blew Ben away! Whooooooosh! As the wind whipped by, he grabbed hold of a table leg and the wind flapped him back and forth as though he were a sheet on a clothesline. Then, just as suddenly, the air grew very still.

Ben peeked from underneath the table. Tongues of fire were touching everyone's head! He rubbed his eyes. Then, all at once, all the grownups began to laugh and hug each other. They all began to dance, and even Aunt Bertharim began to tap her feet. It seemed as if everyone either sang or danced or laughed or cried, all at the same time.

Ben shook his head:

"Hmmm . . . I wonder if this is the Holy Spirit? Could it be? But this doesn't look much like religion—why, everyone is having so much *fun!*"

But then again, maybe this *was* the Holy Spirit. What did he have to lose?

"Lord Jesus, I'm not very old. For now, I can't follow you like my cousin Peter. I can't sell everything and give it to the poor—my father wouldn't let me. But I can *begin* to follow you. As I grow up, I can promise to grow toward you. Could I have just a little of your Holy Spirit?"

A small tongue of fire came down on Ben's head. The little shepherd boy smiled and jumped up from under the table. He took out his windpipe and played a happy tune. All the grownups danced in a circle around him, and that Pentecost proved the happiest Pentecost of his life . . .

Now, it wouldn't be true to say that Ben just lived happily ever after. Every now and then he had a hard day. And Ben still occasionally fought with his little brother. But his life slowly began to change. As Ben grew older, he grew toward God, just as he had promised.

And now when he watched his sheep beneath starlight, the boy shepherd didn't feel lonely anymore. In fact, he almost thought he could hear God's voice whisper from beyond the stars:

"I am the same God who made the sun and the stars and the heavens—and I love you."

No doubt about it. Life was different. And something told Ben that it was the Holy Spirit who made the difference.

ADVENTURES WITH JESUS

"Jesus said, 'Allow the little ones
to come to me and do not hinder them,
for the kingdom of God belongs to such
as these.' "

Matthew 19:14

*The children sit in the family room, waiting for the weekly
radio show to begin. Behind a sheet that is draped over the
dining room chairs, their father sits on the floor. He has an
odd assortment of pots and pans, some of them filled with
water. He switches on a phonograph and begins to speak as
the radio show's theme song begins to play:*

Narrator: "Once again, it is time for the adventures of
'Steve and Beth Ann, Disciples of Jesus.' You remember last
week, when Steve and Beth Ann barely escaped a screaming
mob that had become outraged at the Lord's teachings on
forgiveness. The children pushed their boat out on the Sea of
Galilee with only seconds to spare. They had only a few
scratches and a torn pair of blue jeans. Beth Ann lost a tennis
shoe. It was a very close call. . . ."

Steve: "Whew, Beth Ann! They almost got us that time!
What happened to our Friend?"

Beth Ann: "I don't know. I think I saw him slip through the crowd. Should we head to the other side of the lake?"

Steve: "Take a look at that mob we left behind us. Do we really have a choice? Here—take this side of the sail and I'll pull the rope to lift it up."

The storyteller flaps a pillow case for several seconds, interspersed with exclamations such as "A little higher, Steve!" or, "It's snagged on the masthead, Beth!"

Beth: "Good! The sail is up, and it's caught the wind! Hey! We're really sailing!"

Steve: (worried voice) "Uhmm . . . Beth, I hate to tell you this. But I think we're going to be moving a little *too* fast! Look behind you!"

Beth: "Oh, no! Those black clouds! It's . . . it's a typhoon!

Through the remaining part of the skit: a thin cookie sheet for thunder will do. A watering can sprinkles a thin pan to simulate the sound of rain. These effects build in intensity as the story continues.

Narrator: (melodramatically) "Yes, it was only too true. The worst storm ever seen on the Sea of Galilee raced toward Beth and Steve. The wind howled and the rain fell. The sky was black. The waves swept over the deck of their tiny ship and almost washed them overboard."

Steve: (frantically yelling) "Beth! Are you still hanging on? What are we going to do? Where is our Friend?"

Beth: "I don't know! I think the boat's sprung a leak! Lord Jesus, where are you?"

Steve: "Wait! Wait! I think I see someone walking across the water. But it looks—oh, no! It looks like a ghost! That's all we need now!"

Beth: "A ghost? Where? Yes . . . yes. . . I see it! But wait!

91

I don't think it's a ghost. It looks that way because of the storm! I think it's the Lord!"

Steve: "Lord, if it's you, tell us to come across the water!"

Jesus: (calm, soothing voice) "Come this way, Beth. Come this way, Steve. Don't be afraid."

Beth: "Steve, hold my hand as we step out. This is scary . . . but . . . it's working! We can walk on the water!"

Steve: "You're right! It's a little like skating. But wait! My feet are getting wet! The Lord's saying something. What's he saying? I can't quite hear him over the wind! We're sinking! Help!"

Beth: "He's saying something about keeping our eyes on him. At least, I think that's what he's saying. But when you're sinking, how can you do anything but look at the water? We're going down! Help! Help!"

The storyteller speaks in a grim voice as he switches on the show's theme song:

Narrator: "It was only too true. The water rose up to their knees and then up to their waists. The waves roared and the wind howled. What would become of them? Would their Friend help them in time? Would they be saved from the stormy waters? They're sinking fast. Tune in next week, for the continuing adventures of 'Steve and Beth Ann: Disciples of Jesus.' "

THE INNKEEPER OF BETHLEHEM

"She wrapped him in cloth and
set him in a manger, because there was
no room for him at the inn."

Luke 2:7

*The teacher backs slowly into his classroom with a sheet
draped over his head and shoulders. A cord ties it around his
forehead, giving it a turbaned effect. He yells impatiently to
someone outside the door:*

"I already told you, Matthias—there's no more room! I
can't do anything about it! Where could we sleep them? On
the window sills?"

*He mutters unhappily to himself. But then he notices the
children in the room.*

"Oh! Sorry, I didn't know anyone was here. Do you
have a bed for the night? Well, you're lucky. A lot of people
don't. Ever since the emperor called that stupid census, I've
been going crazy. This inn has turned into a madhouse. Say,
do you mind if I rest for a few minutes?"

He sits down in front of the blackboard and whispers:

"That emperor is stupid! Just don't tell anyone that I said it—I don't want to get my head cut off! First, he wants to count everyone in the empire. And, of course, in Judea that means that everyone's got to go back to the family's hometown. But Bethlehem is a small town! We can't handle this many travelers!"

The teacher-turned-innkeeper pounds his staff on the floor. Then he grows more thoughtful.

"Like last night—it almost broke my heart. The inn was filled up, with hardly room to breathe. And then this knock came on the door. A young couple stood there. The young man's name was Jacob or Joseph or something. I forget his wife's name. They came from some backwater town up north by the big lake.

"She was going to have a baby. I wish there'd have been some room, but where could I have put them? Finally, they went up the hillside to the stables."

He sighs and shakes his head.

"For some reason, their faces haunted me. I tried to get some sleep that night, but I just tossed and turned. At last, I got out of bed and went to the window."

He walks to the classroom window and points out toward imaginary hills.

"You wouldn't believe what I saw! A star! It lit up the whole valley and the whole hillside! I climbed into my clothes and stumbled downstairs. The star was directly over the stable where that young girl was having her baby. . . ."

"Well, my feet took me as quickly as they could to the

stable. I heard the goats bleating and the cattle lowing and the chickens peeping. Then what do you think happened? Just as I got to the stable door, a bunch of dirty shepherds ran out and almost knocked me over!

" 'A beautiful baby!' they were shouting. 'The angel was right! I wouldn't have believed it if I hadn't seen it myself!' These shepherds, I thought to myself, might do better if they minded their sheepskins and stayed away from their wine-skins.

"But after they left, I walked into the stable. The night grew very quiet. In the hay, beside the light of a small oil lamp, the young woman was lying with her little baby. Now, I'm a sensible man. Why did I get up in the middle of the night for some baby born in a stable? I'm not sure.

"But you know, most of the news that we hear nowadays sounds pretty bad. There's a war here and a disaster there. But something tells me when that baby grows up, he's going to do something special. And—if we give him half a chance—who knows? He might change some of that bad news into happy news!"

The innkeeper turns toward the door as though he's listening to someone.

"What's that, Matthias? We're out of blankets? Didn't you do the laundry yesterday? Do I have to do everything around here myself?"

He pounds his staff on the floor as he walks out the door.

TELLING OUR FIRST STORY

After reading these stories, two voices may jostle inside of us. One says:

"Storytelling *is* a beautiful way to share life with others. For my church, for my students, for my family—why don't I become a storyteller?"

But then the second voice grumbles. Its quiet gnawing leaves us with an uneasy feeling:

"You'd just make a fool of yourself. Look at the length of those stories—remember how much trouble you had with a few verses of Shakespeare in high school? . . . Besides, you haven't time. It's far too much trouble."

This second voice just doesn't know what it's talking about. Storytelling is not hard, grueling work. It requires surprisingly little memorization. (After all, we're not producing a Broadway play!) Its preparation flows naturally, and can even prove exhilarating fun.

Let's take the story about that poor streetsweeper who lived in the shining days of knighthood. Step-by-step, we again experience storytelling as a unique adventure—and as a coming-home.

1. Relax and read the story aloud to yourself.

Get away alone and find your favorite chair. Forget about trying to memorize anything. Notice, as you read it aloud, how much more alive it becomes when it's spoken.

2. Now ask yourself: Why would I want to tell this story?

Sometimes we just tell a story for the sheer enjoyment. But in ministry, we need to grasp clearly why we are telling it—what our purpose is. What are we trying to communicate? It deeply helps our storytelling if we can identify the experience of the story with something in our own life. This takes the question "Why am I telling this story?" and moves it onto a much more personal plane.

Do Sam's experiences resemble any of your own? In your Christian life, have you ever worked hard for a white wedding suit? Have you ever fallen in a mud-puddle? Did you ever have to decide whether to go into a wedding feast dripping with mud?

On a personal level, what is the one central point of the story that you want to communicate?

3. Imagine your listeners sitting in front of you.

No one prepares a gift without knowing for whom they make it. Ask yourself: With whom do I really want to share this story? Perhaps there comes to mind a typical American congregation that works itself to death for white wedding suits . . . or a group of divorced singles who are struggling through the mud-puddle of a broken marriage, . . . or a group of teens trying to understand the Christian decision. From this point onward, imagine that they are listening to your preparations.

4. Now, in a minute or less, briefly sum up the story's plot.

Speak aloud, and pretend you are talking to those imaginary listeners who sit around the room . . .

Good. At first you might have felt awkward—but now you have the kernel of the story. I would summarize the plot of Sam's story in this way:

"Long ago in the days of knighthood, there lived a poor streetsweeper named Sam. He lived in a shack and hated himself. But then one day the prince of his city decided to become his friend, and Sam began to change.

"After a while, the prince even invited Sam to come to his wedding. The poor streetsweeper worked hard to buy a white wedding suit. But when the day of the wedding actually came, Sam fell into a huge mud-puddle. Did Sam trust the prince's friendship enough to go into the feast? Would you go into that castle dripping with mud?"

A summary of the plot takes perhaps forty seconds—that's not too difficult. Notice how, when you summarized the plot, it forced you into your own natural speech patterns. That's exactly what is needed. Never try to tell a story word for word as it is written. It is an ancient privilege of storytellers that they can retell any story in their own words. We even hear of the age-old blessing of the Irish storyteller, who would say at his story's end:

"And may the next one who tells it— better it!"

Once again, in your own words, very briefly sum up the story's plot.

5. Next, we will take our imaginary audience on a guided tour of the story's world.

Here we encounter a key to good storytelling. A story is always told from the "inside" looking out. When we tell of

Sam standing in front of his cracked mirror, we actually imagine ourselves standing in his dirty, cluttered shack. Or with the story of the puddle-fish, the area in front of our classroom blackboard actually becomes a small puddle of water. And we tell the story from within its waters. We are *in* the story and not merely telling about it. This brings the story incredibly alive. Your listeners will be drawn into the story's world and forget about themselves. (And, incidentally, they will also forget about their defenses!)

How can we most easily develop a knack for telling a story from within? Let's read the story aloud once again and, as we read, stop here and there for an exercise with our imaginations. When you come across the description of a setting, stop reading. Remember how you used to make-believe when you were a child? Do that now. Get up from your chair and close your eyes. When you open them again you no longer stand in your own bedroom. You stand on the drawbridge of a medieval castle, walking into the story's world.

Stroll around. Feel the hard stone walls. Wander into the castle courtyard, all the time describing out loud what you see, smell, touch and hear. Imagine that you are giving a guided tour to your listeners. Yes, it's very true—if people walked into the room at this moment, they'd think you were crazy. But be a child and have *fun* with the story. Your words might sound something like this:

"This is great! I've always wanted to tour a medieval walled city. (It sure beats Pittsburgh.) This drawbridge looks like it's hewn out of oak . . . And the cobble-stoned streets are certainly narrow—ooops! That knight on horseback almost ran me down! Why doesn't he watch where he's driving? . . . Why look! There's Sam's shack! What a dump. It's leaning against that old stone wall, made out of nothing but old boards, and a leaky tin roof . . ."

It wouldn't even hurt if we knelt down to inspect Sam's mud-puddle: "Hmmm. It looks about an inch deep. Brown soupy water on the top, and black oozy muck on the bottom. Not a pleasant place to land head-first."

Now, on your own, give a guided tour of Sam's world as you read through the story . . .

Welcome back to the twentieth century. At this point, you begin to be on the *inside* of the story, rather than looking at it from the outside. And, as you experience the story's world, any need for memorization shrinks toward insignificance.

But this also would be a good place for warning. While we must be familiar with the story's world, we must beware of bogging down in too much description. Our descriptions of setting and characters must be concise.

Action is the real focus of a good story. Our brief descriptions create only the empty frame into which we place the real heart of our story—its action. For example, take the story of "Ananias the Shoemaker." This story's lively action describes more than ten pages of character analysis—and it keeps our listeners captivated. With trembling knees, Ananias knocks on the rich man's house. And then the struggle begins—with the timid shoemaker pushing past the angry servant, the doorkeeper planting his hand in Ananias' face and slamming the door, the shoemaker screaming and struggling until, at last, a voice cries from the inner courtyard:

"Wait! I had a vision about than man!"

Now that we have become familiar with the story's setting, we have our frame. In a few moments, let's learn how to paint our story with bold and colorful strokes.

6. Once more for review, tell the story-plot to your listeners.

Notice how it's beginning to flow more naturally. You relate something experienced rather than memorized . . .

7. Now we enflesh the story's action—by climbing inside its characters.

We read through our story for a third time. Action flows out of the story's characters, and therefore we need to get within them. Our doorway lies through the use of direct quotes.

As you read through the story, stop at each quote. For example, stand in front of Sam's cracked mirror and take a long look at yourself. Then say:

"Lord, the day you made me—you sure made a mistake!"

Obviously, we never actually storytell the descriptive phrase that precedes or follows a quote (such as "He sighed, shaking his head"). These descriptions must be included on a printed page, but they come alive only in the storyteller's voice, face, and body movements.

There is an excellent method for loosening up. Say the direct quote three times. First, say it in the dullest possible monotone. (Yes! The most horribly insipid monotone that you can imagine.) Be sure that you stand stiff as a board, with zero facial expression . . .

Good. Now go to the other extreme and become as melodramatic as possible. Let loose—with your voice and your entire body! It should be a ridiculous caricature of the appropriate emotion. Have some fun and be a fool for Christ . . .

Very good. Since you've hit both extremes, it should be fairly easy to hit the appropriate middle-ground. (By the way, when someone first begins storytelling, the "appropriate middle-ground" is often identical with our "melodramatic" rendition. It takes a little time for us to really loosen up.)

Now read through the entire story and use this method

101

on each direct quote. Use your voice, your face, your hands. your entire body. You become the characters of that medieval walled city . . .

8. We now take notice of the rhythms and the silences that are embedded in good storytelling.

We must be aware of the simple rhythms that flow through many of our stories. These most often take the form of key phrases or sentences which repeat themselves at appropriate intervals. As you've certainly noticed, the story about our poor streetsweeper has an obvious example. Several times we find ourselves repeating with a smile the familiar description of his wedding suit:

" . . . a white shirt and a white coat and white pants and white socks and white shoes. Not to mention white suspenders with imitation diamonds which spelled, "S-A-M."

The steady, smiling repetition of these words slowly builds toward the dramatic climax of the story, when Sam falls—*splat!*—into the mud-puddle. Without this steady build-up, the story's *impact* falls instead into the muck.

The final line of "Once Upon a Puddle" is very similar. It has been repeated throughout the story several times, building to a dramatic end: "And so, once again, they began to swim in circles and hunt for waterbugs." So also with the final, solemn ending of the "Parable of the Lighthouse." And we find the climax of "Barnaby the Juggler" comes just after he repeats his opening announcement:

"Ladies and gentlemen of heaven, my name is Barnaby, and the best thing I do in all the world . . ." As the old familiar lines come around, our listeners smile with delight. Let these phrases be in your own words, but never leave them out. Without them, many stories will sound as off-key as a musician's worst nightmare.

Besides this internal rhythm, we must use silence for

good storytelling. At a story's beginning, few things can prepare an audience better than silence. (Silent prayer can work even better.) And, obviously, dramatic pauses heighten a story's impact when they are interwoven through its telling.

Ironically, one of the most common sins against good storytelling is perpetrated *after* the story is over. Instead of standing still and holding the silence at the story's end, storytellers often abruptly walk away. This distracts our listeners and does violence to their personal reflections on the story's meaning.

As you begin to tell stories, freely experiment with silence. Often, it can say more than a thousand words.

9. Next, practice actually telling the story to your imaginary listeners.

Before you begin, accept the fact that you will make mistakes. You will stumble in a few places. Mistakes themselves do not greatly detract from a good story—rather, what detracts is our own negative reaction to the mistake. The audience cringes when it sees our embarrassment. If we take our error in stride, then so will our listeners. (My best storytelling sessions have been where I've made a few mistakes. People enjoy hearing a real flesh-and-blood person, not a "storytelling-machine.")

As you tell your story, remember—enthusiasm covers a multitude of mistakes . . .

10. At last, you are ready to tell your first story.

"What! But we've only practiced it once!"

That's right, but once again, we're not preparing a Broadway play. Storytelling needs that spontaneous rustic quality, and too much rehearsal dampens this.

Ultimately, our storytelling potential only emerges when

we stand in front of real people. It takes a small measure of humility, but the best way to learn is simply to *do* it, just as the day when I told that first ragged story of Brother Juniper.

As the ancient Irish storytellers would say:

"May the next one of you who tells these stories—better them!"

With the help of that storyteller who walked along the water's edge, I'm certain you will.

APPENDIX

USES WITH EVANGELISM, LECTIONARIES, AND RENEWAL PROGRAMS

This brief appendix is a reference help to the busy minister or teacher who:

1. needs a story to illustrate a particular Gospel passage,
2. seeks a story to parallel a particular Sunday lectionary reading, or
3. needs a story to enliven a specific church renewal program.

Notice that throughout the years many different occasions may arise to tell the same story. Even with the same audience, this is not necessarily bad—in fact, occasional repetition is highly recommended. Like a good song, a good story grows each time we experience it.

I. Stories for Use with the Synoptic Gospels

Theme	Gospel	Story
Nativity	Mt 1:18–24 Lk 2:1–7	Stable Glimpse, Barnaby, Innkeeper, Prodigal Father
Search of Magi	Mt 2:1–12	Once Upon Puddle, Barnaby
Preaching of John	Mk 1:1–18 Mt 3:1–12 Lk 3:1–18	Once Upon Puddle, Seed Story, Rich Man and Lazarus
Jesus Calls the Fishermen	Mt 4:18–21 Mk 1:16–20 Lk 5:1–11	Seed Story, Puddle
Beatitudes	Mt 5:1–11 Lk 6:20–23	Ananias, Seed Story, Happy Man's Shirt
Light of the World	Mt 5:13–16 Mk 9:50 Lk 14:34–35	Lighthouse Parable
Love of Enemies	Mt 5:38–48 Lk 6:27–28, 32–36	Samaritan, Lord When?
Riches in Heaven	Mt 6:19–21, 24–34 Lk 12:22–31, 33–34	Unless Seed Die, Happy Man's Shirt, Rich Man and Lazarus
Faith of Centurion	Mt 8:5–13 Lk 7:1–10	Streetsweeper
Would-Be Followers	Mt 8:18–22 Lk 9:57–62	Unless Seed Die, Puddle

Calms a Storm	Mt 8:23–27 Mk 4:35–41 Lk 8:22–25	Walking with Lord, Adventures with Jesus
Mission of Twelve	Mt 10:5–15 Mk 6:7–13 Lk 9:1–6	Lighthouse Parable
Loving God More Than Family	Mt 10:34–39 Lk 12:51–53 14:26–27	Wedding Story
Take My Yoke	Mt 11:28–30	Walking with Lord
Peter Walks on Water	Mt 6:45–52	Streetsweeper, Walking with Lord, Adventures with Jesus
Leaving God's Will for Own	Mt 15:1–9 Mk 7:1–13	Samaritan, Lighthouse
Jesus Speaks of His Passion	Mt 16:21–28 Mk 8:31–9:1 Lk 9:22–27	Father's Love, Unless Seed Die
Transfiguration	Mt 17:1–8 Mk 9:2–13 Lk 9:28–36	Stable Glimpse, Prodigal Father
Being as a Child	Mt 18:1–4 19:13–15 Mk 9:33–37 Lk 9:46–48	Barnaby
Rich Young Man	Mt 19:16–22 Mk 10:17–31 Lk 18:18–30	Once Upon Puddle, Unless Seed Die, Rich Man and Lazarus
Rich Entering the Kingdom	Mt 19:23–26 Mk 10:23–27 Lk 18:24–27	Happy Man's Shirt, Rich Man and Lazarus

Least Is Greatest	Mt 20:20–28 Mk 10:35–45	Barnaby, Ananias
Great Commandment	Mt 22:34–40 Mk 12:28–34 Lk 10:25–28	Wedding Story
No One Knows Hour	Mt 24:36–44 Mk 13:32–37 Lk 17:26–30	Very Last Day
Last Judgment	Mt 25:31–46	Lord When?, Rich Man and Lazarus
Passion Narrative	Mt 26:1– 27:66 Mk 14:1– 15:47 Lk 22:1–23:56	Unless Seed Die, Father's Love
Resurrection	Mt 28:1–15 Mk 16:1–10 Lk 24:1–12	Unless Seed Die, Father's Love, Prodigal Father
Final Commission of Apostles	Mt 28:16–20 Mk 16:14–18 Lk 24:36–49	Lighthouse Parable, Ananias, Lord When?
Annuciation	Lk 1:26–38	Wedding Story
Mary's Song	Lk 1:46–55	Ananias, Barnaby, Streetsweeper
Preaching Gospel to the Poor	Mt 13:53–58 Lk 4:16–30	Lighthouse Parable
In House of Simon the Pharisee	Lk 7:36–50	Barnaby

Martha and Mary	Lk 10:38–42	Walking with Lord
Zacchaeus	Lk 19:1–10	Once Upon Puddle, Unless Seed Die, Walking with Lord, Rich Man and Lazarus
Widow's Offering	Lk 21:1–4	Barnaby

II. Stories for Use with the Sunday Lectionary†

Holy Days

Christmas	Stable Glimpse, Wedding Story, Father's Love, Prodigal Father, Innkeeper
Holy Family	Wedding Story
Holy Week	Father's Love, Unless Seed Die
Easter	Father's Love, Prodigal Father
Ascension	Parable of Lighthouse
Pentecost	Little Boy's Pentecost

Sunday of Year	Cycle A	Cycle B	Cycle C
1st of Advent	Very Last Day	Lighthouse	Very Last Day
4th of Advent	Stable Glimpse	Stable Glimpse	Wedding Story
2nd of Easter	Upon a Puddle, Prodigal Father	Lighthouse, Prodigal Father	*
3rd of Easter	Prodigal Father	*	Lord, When?, Prodigal Father
4th of Easter	Upon a Puddle	Father's Love, Prodigal Father	Upon a Puddle
5th of Easter	Streetsweeper	*	Samaritan, Lord When?
6th of Easter	*	Father's Love, Lord, When?	Walking with Lord
2nd Ordinary or 2nd Epiphany	*	Ananias	*

3rd Ordinary
or 3rd Epiphany .... Lighthouse .... Upon a Puddle .... *

4th Ordinary
or 4th Epiphany .... Ananias, Barnaby, ... * ... Streetsweeper, Prodigal Father
Streetsweeper, Prodigal Father

5th Ordinary
or 5th Epiphany .... Lord When?, Rich Man Lazarus .... * ... Streetsweeper, Prodigal Father

6th Ordinary
or 6th Epiphany .... * .... * ... Happy Man's Shirt, Rich Man and Lazarus .....

7th Ordinary
or 7th Epiphany .... Samaritan, Unforgiving Servant .... * ... Samaritan, Unforgiving Servant

8th Ordinary
or 8th Epiphany .... Happy Man's Shirt, Rich Man and Lazarus .... * ... Very Last Day, Unforgiving Servant

11th Ordinary
or 4th Pentecost .... Streetsweeper, Prodigal Father .. Ananias .... *

12th Ordinary
or 5th Pentecost .... Stable Glimpse ... Walking with Lord .... Unless Seed Die

13th Ordinary
or 6th Pentecost .... Unless Seed Die ... Samaritan, Lord When? .... *

14th Ordinary
or 7th Pentecost .... Walking with Lord ... * .... Lighthouse

15th Ordinary
or 8th Pentecost .... * ... Lighthouse .... Samaritan

16th Ordinary
or 9th Pentecost .... * .... Walking with Lord ....

17th Ordinary
or 10th Pentecost .... * ....Father's Love, Prodigal Father

18th Ordinary
or 11th Pentecost .... * ....Unless Seed Die, Happy Man's Shirt, Rich Man and Lazarus ....

19th Ordinary
or 12th Pentecost .. Walking with Lord .... * .... Very Last Day, Rich Man and Lazarus ....
Adventures with Jesus

21st Ordinary
or 14th Pentecost .... * ....Once Upon Puddle, Rich Man and Lazarus ....

22nd Ordinary
or 15th Pentecost .. Unless a Seed Die, ... * ....Ananias, Barnaby, Streetsweeper, Rich Man and Lazarus ....
Prodigal Father

23rd Ordinary
or 16th Pentecost ....Ananias, Barnaby .... * ....Unless a Seed Die ....

24th Ordinary
or 17th Pentecost .. Samaritan, Unforgiving Servant .. Lord When? .... *

25th Ordinary
or 18th Pentecost .. Barnaby .... * ....Happy Man's Shirt, Rich Man and Lazarus ....

26th Ordinary		
or 19th Pentecost	.. Lighthouse .... Unless Seed Die, ... Lord When?	
	Happy Man's Shirt,	
	Rich Man and Lazarus ...... Rich Man and Lazarus	
27th Ordinary		
or 20th Pentecost	.... * .... Barnaby .... *	
28th Ordinary		
or 21st Pentecost	.. Streetsweeper ...... Once Upon Puddle, ... *	
	Rich Man and Lazarus	
29th Ordinary		
or 22nd Pentecost	.... * .... Unless Seed Die .... *	
30th Ordinary		
or 23rd Pentecost	.. Wedding Story ...... * .... *	
31st Ordinary		
or 24th Pentecost	.... * .... Wedding Story ...... Barnaby	
32nd Ordinary		
or 25th Pentecost	.. Very Last Day, Rich Man ...... Barnaby .... *	
	and Lazarus	
Last Ordinary		
or last Pentecost	... Lord When?, Unforgiving Servant, ... * .... *	
	Rich Man and Lazarus	

†This chart comes from a survey of the Roman Catholic lectionary. It is accurate also for use by Episcopal, Lutheran, United Methodist, and Presbyterian/U.C.C. Significant differences between the five lectionaries proved rare, and separate charts for each would be more awkward than helpful.

III. Renewal Programs

Roman Catholic:

1. Cursillo.

Night of arrival:
First meditation: Very Last Day
Third meditation: Once Upon Puddle, Unless
Seed Die, or Streetsweeper

First day:
Talk #2: Streetsweeper
Talk #3: Parable of Lighthouse
Talk #4: Ananias, or Parable of Lighthouse
Talk #5: Mary as Mother

Second day:
Talk #6: Glimpse into Stable
Talk #7: Glimpse into Stable
Talk #8: Ananias, Samaritan, or Lord When?
Talk #9: Once Upon Puddle, Unless Seed Die
Talk #10: Ananias

Third day:
Fifth meditation: Once Upon a Puddle
Talk #11: Ananias
Talk #13: Parable of Lighthouse, or Lord When?
Talk #15: Once Upon Puddle, Ananias,
Lighthouse

2. Life in the Spirit Seminars.

>   Seminar #1: Streetsweeper
>   Seminar #2: Glimpse into Stable, Father's Love
>   Seminar #3: Once Upon a Puddle, Unless Seed
>   Die, Father's Love
>   Seminar #6: Once Upon a Puddle